The Unauthorized Ubiquiti Routing and Switching Manual - Volume 1

by

Kevin Houser and Eric Weber

Printed in the United States of America

First Printing, 2018

ISBN 978-1-977088-36-9

An Acknowledgment

Thanks.

I would like to graciously thank my very good friend and Mentor in all things proper, Eric Weber. Without his firm hand and guidance I would never have been able to present this material. I would also like to thank all of the great people at Microcom in Calabasas CA.

I would of course also like to thank all of the great people at Ubiquiti, for creating the amazing product lines, and the almost too good to be true pricing model, that not only serves the underserved, but the Non-served as well.

Lastly I want to thank all the students that I have had the pleasure of getting to know. I never have a Training class where I learn nothing. I always want to stay in the mode of learning and discovery. And it's the students and their own broad and varied background that helps me in the next class. Thanks to you all.

Comments or questions are encouraged. Feel free to send an email, snarky, nice or otherwise to contact@therouterbook.com. I might even send a snarky reply. You can also visit our website www.therouterbook.com. For those of you in need of training, go to www.microcom.us, or to www.web-er.com/training.

Introduction

My name is Kevin Houser, and I am currently a Fulltime trainer. The reason for this text is to aid students and others who may not be fully versed in the language of Routing and Switching. This should be regarded as an Entry-Level Text.

This text is not the complete manual. It does not include every possible command in the CLI, or even every option in the Graphical interface. What it will do is attempt to translate some of the technical into actual plain English. It is also an introductory text on Networking. With chapters devoted to IP addressing and Switching Basics.

Ubiquiti offers an introductory class that is called the UBRSS. It is a three day class that is designed to introduce the student to the Edge Router. I feel that this text is the unofficial companion for that class.

I have attempted to include the WHY. I like why. It seems to be invisible in most texts. When a text instructs you to do X, instead of Y, It's nice to have the reasoning behind it. I think it also allows for a learning opportunity, to have the understanding of choosing X over Y, and being able to apply that understanding to other platforms, and frankly to any other project you may be involved with.

Oh, and one more thing. The reason the title of the text is The Unauthorized Ubiquiti Routing and Switching Manual, is well, it's just that. Unauthorized. Nobody said,"Hey Kevin, please write a book." I felt there was a need for it. So here it is.

TABLE OF CONTENTS

Chapter 1

THE OSI REFERENCE MODEL

I have read quite the number of Technical tomes, and, they mostly suck. Now I know that may not be proper usage of the work suck, but highly technical books just do. They suck. I have read some of these books and they can easily replace sleeping pills, so, of course I want to start you off on your journey to better understand Routing and Switching by introducing you to the OSI reference model. To say that this stuff is a little dry is really an understatement. I want you to understand that I will try to give you the stuff you need to know, and have it make sense, without sucking.

The Model itself was put together; I am sure, for several reasons, but you will need to know what it is, why it's structured the way it is, and how it relates to Routing and Switching.

What it is.

Well, it's a paradigm, or model to help us better understand the innards of data flow, and the use of various networking devices. You remember, those routers and switches that are stacked up in the computer room. In plain terms it is a technique to break down a complex procedure, and to break it down into seven chunks that will be slightly easier to digest.

LAYER 1: THE PHYSICAL LAYER

Welcome to layer one. This layer is there to deal with the signaling and wiring standards. Data at this layer is represented by BITS. These little guys known as BITS or binary digits have to be represented by something. And that's the function of this layer. To have a certain amount of voltage to be representing a Binary 1, or a certain amount representing a binary 0, is what is happening here.

Let's get real basic. A binary one (1), is usually referred to as the ON bit. While 0 becomes the OFF bit. You can think of them as True/False, On/Off, Yes/No. It is here at layer one where we have standards to sort all that out. So there are standards written for cable at this layer. If you have ever run Ethernet cables, you may have had to install connectors on this cable. And someone may have told you that there were distance limitations to follow. Well, that's what these standards at this layer are there for. They have spent lots of time with slide rules and heavy-duty pocket protectors to create all those exciting rules, so follow the rules. Use the correct connectors. Do not run Ethernet cables beyond what the standards tell you to run it. If you are old enough to remember things like 10Base2 or 10Base5, there were rules at layer one that told you how far you could run a 10Base5 cable. The number 5 represented 500 meters as a maximum distance. For 10Base2 it was 185 meters. For twisted pair Ethernet the maximum distance is 100 meters.

More basics; Layer one also deals with hardware such as cables and connectors. The Physical connectors that make up the media itself. Devices at this layer include the actual cable itself, also known as media. It also includes the devices known as hubs. You don't find this device anymore, as they have been replaced by the more adept and flexible switch.

Why do you need to know this? As a Network/IT person, you may be looking at a troubleshooting scenario. Someone may ask you if you have a physical or a Layer one problem. What are they really saying? They are saying, "Hey is the wire plugged in? Is it the correct wire?" That's the physical layer. Well that's enough of that. Let's move on.

LAYER 2: THE DATA-LINK LAYER

The Data-Link layer is responsible for organizing all those voltage or light pulses from layer one into some form of organization. At this layer we have frames and we have a few other things that not only organize these bits into a framework, but there are also mechanisms in place to check to see if there are any errors in certain areas of the frame. Okay, not to get too crazy here but let's look at a few things that are specific to this layer.

Thing one is framing. All our bits are going to be placed in a frame, so we can sort out which bits represent what information. These frames are very precise in size so it makes things much more manageable for other Layer Two devices to move the data along throughout the Local Area Network (LAN).

Thing 2 is physical addressing. At layer 2 we have physical addressing. That means we can identify devices on our local area network as unique devices. Your PC has a network interface adapter, and that adapter is identified with a physical address, known as a MAC address. Therefore, your PC is unique in your network. The MAC address that it uses is encoded onto the card itself. It is unique to the card, and is similar to you having a Social Security number. It is unique to you.

Thing 3 is flow control. Slow down. That's flow control.

Coming in at number 4 we have error control. In a frame we have very precise fields, and part of that is a way to identify errors. At the end of a frame there is a trailer, an end part that says something like; "this frame is this number sequence." It could be something like frame one of a billion. Frames also contain information on frame sizes. So, if there is any kind of bits not getting in line correctly, or trying to arrive out of sequence, we can check that information out in our trailer area of the frame itself. And if there is an error, we can dump that frame and get a new one. We also have protocols at this layer that keep track of fun stuff like access control.

Now before I go too far too fast. I used a word you may not fully understand. The word "Protocol." You may have heard it thrown around like a journeyman wrestler on a Saturday night. For now, just think of the word protocol as a rule for some kind of communication. You may have heard of TCP, and yes, it is a protocol, and yes, it is full of rules for communicating. More on TCP a little later.

At Layer two, our data, all those bits, are placed into a framework. A frame that can be identified as part of a conversation between devices on the same Local Area Network. There are different frame types, but for now, just stick with the idea of data in an organized container, where both the source of the frame, and the destination are identified with a physical address. One for the sender, and another for the receiver. The Data-Link layer is doing all this frame stuff and addressing stuff, so when we have a connection from device to device, through a switch, the switch itself can read the frame and know what to do with it. So a switch is a layer 2 device. Some may tell you fanciful stories of switches that operate at layer 3 or 4 or even layer 7. While that may be true, it's not the norm. For now, just think of switches as layer 2 devices. It moves data along based on the MAC address of the receiver. It does not deliver data based on the IP address.

Protocols at this layer include ARP, which is Address Resolution Protocol. This guy is responsible for finding a layer 2 address, which is a 48 Bit MAC address that is written in Hexadecimal format. It will do this for a local device. Other protocols include Virtual LAN (VLAN), which allows the creation of additional, separate LANS from a switch perspective. There are many more but the big daddy at Layer 2 is Ethernet. You probably thought it was just related to the concept of networking, but nope. Ethernet tells us the rules we have to help us gain access to the wire, or physical layer, from our Layer two devices.

Ok, let's review. Data at Layer two is in the form of a frame. Devices here are Layer two switches, and network adapters. You know network adapters, they are the things into which we plug the Ethernet cables. Remember that the Network Interface Card has a physical address that does not change. That would be the MAC address.

Why do you need to know this? Think of an entire room full of computers. They all connect to a switch to allow them to communicate with each other. They connect us with local resources like printers or copy machines. At Layer 2, they get to move data locally through that speedy switch.

If the switch were to fail, we would have a layer 2 problem. Layer 2 affects all the computers or other devices connected this way. Your switch actually learns what MAC address is on every physical port. More fun stuff later on what some switches can do for us. Switches are covered in Chapter 4. Moving on.

LAYER 3: THE NETWORK LAYER

This fun-filled layer is responsible for moving Packets. This is the form of the data at this layer. The device that handles that data transfer is a router. This layer has the big job of moving data from your network to another network. That network is often called The Wide Area Network, or WAN. In most American homes you will find a device, forced upon you by your ISP (Internet Service Provider), some will call it a modem, some call it a router, and some call it horrible names, as it can become cranky and unreliable at times. It's the device that tech support at the ISP always asks you; "Have you tried unplugging it and plugging it back in?"

Whatever you call it, the router is actually doing some layer 3 stuff, as it is moving data from your network, onto the Service Provider's network. To be able to do all that movement of data, the router has to understand the destination of the packet. The destination in this case, is not the MAC address we had at layer 2, but it is an IP address. The difference between the IP address and the Mac address is pretty basic. IP version 4, the current version in use, is a 32 bit long address that identifies your devices in a different way than the MAC address does. For starters it looks like this: 192.168.10.105. While the Mac address looks like AE:1F:32:09:71:33.

The IP address is written in decimal notation, while the MAC address is written as a HEX number. The HEX number is actually 48 bits long. The router does not look at the MAC address to "route" the packet. The router needs the IP address.

The Protocols that work at this layer are numerous, but for now we will just look at a few major ones. IPv4 along with IPv6 operate here, and they identify devices with either a 32 bit address (v4) or a 128 bit address (v6). Complete understanding of the workings and mysteries of IPv6 are not covered in this text. Should you find yourself having trouble sleeping, I am sure you can "Google" IPv6. The devices we will be using are mainly configured as IPv4 devices. IPv4 will be covered a little later in much more depth.

Since this layer is responsible for routing, we also have routing protocols here at layer three such as OSPF, RIP, IGRP, and several more. These routing protocols determine the best direction to move the data across the internet using their own internal algorithms.

Why do you need to know this? Well the routing process can become very complex, and it will help if we have a better understanding of what makes it work. Even if we are only setting up Uncle Larry's internet for him, it is helpful to understand that Uncle Larry's house is the LAN, and he wants to connect to the internet to read his email, and that internet is the WAN. He connects to an ISP, or service provider's network to get out onto the web, where he can then use Google to search for "IPv6," since he drinks too much coffee and has trouble falling asleep. Moving on.

LAYER 4: THE TRANSPORT LAYER

The Transport layer is tasked with providing host to host transport of data. That's sounds pretty easy right? The transport layer uses TCP, or it can use UDP, as its main protocols. The difference is considerable. TCP is regarded as a Connection-Oriented protocol. In very basic terms, that means there is an internal mechanism that keeps track of sending data, and then finding out if the receiver got that particular piece of information. TCP uses ACK's or acknowledgments, along with a few friends to sort out if the data is being received or not. Computer A will send a group of packets or "Data" to computer B. Then A will say; "Hey, did you get that data I sent you?" And if everything is working correctly then B will say; "Yes I got that, send more."

All the happy little packets are identified as well, so if one goes missing, that one can be resent. Data at this layer would be termed as a segment. Segments are lots of packets lumped together. TCP is considered to be reliable due to the error control mechanisms that are being used. The drawback to all this great reliable, connection oriented fun, is that all that asking; "Did you get that?", and answering; "Yes I did, send some more." It is not a very efficient use of the bandwidth. The ACK's are not part of the data that we want, but they are a part of the overhead that we may not need.

The other protocol at this layer is UDP. It is not a connection-oriented protocol. It is considered Connection-less. There is no mechanism for UDP to find out if the receiver actually got the data that was sent. There are no ACK's, so, of course this sounds bad, right?

"Not reliable," that is not something I am putting on my singles profile. "Likes long moonlit walks on the beach," or, "likes cats," yes, but "not reliable," not so much. Not to fear. First off, for some types of data that is being used today, we just don't have time to wait for the "did you get that stuff I sent?" "Yes I did," response. Some things like a VOIP phone call or a video that you are streaming off the internet can use UDP.

This type of data must be sent without any delay, or the phone call may be full of errors, like Jitter, which is not a good thing to have on an important phone call. "Have you tried unplugging it, and plugging it back in?" Now that's an important phone call.

I like to think of Layer 4 as the UPS delivery warehouse. All of the boxes and packages that are going to be delivered are identified with an address. If the box is going to your house then there is a label on the box with your address. It's almost like an IP address. All the boxes are identified with a label that may also have something like box 2 of 100.

The Transport layer also identifies packets with a sequence number, so if you were missing one of the boxes, it would be easy to know which one to request. "Hey, I am missing box 45, resend it please." To be very technical, there are actually two sequence numbers that are used. One side of the connection will choose this number at random, and this is a good thing for the security minded individual. The first sequence number identifies where in the data stream, the packet actually is, and the second is an ACK sequence that identifies how many packets have been received. Both of these sequence numbers are offset by the starting sequence number.

While this may help you understand what is really going on here, you also need to realize that the UPS warehouse hands those packages off to a delivery driver to get it to your home. That delivery van is just like a layer three router that has the task of delivering the boxes, or packets, directly, based upon the route that the particular driver knows. This is the same thing as your router. He also has a route to get packets where they have to be. It makes perfect sense, right?

Layer 4 is responsible for Flow control and Error correction. Error correction makes sense here because all the packets are identified, so it would seem pretty easy to recover from a lost packet. But wait, UDP doesn't have all that ACK stuff going on, so how do we recover from an error? To answer that question, let's visit the past.

Once upon a time, back in the dark ages of computing, engineers were tasked with creating standards and protocols that could move data in a reliable way from one place to another. You have to understand that at the time, there was no software in place, so the communication at this layer had to be created from scratch. The idea to use a form of acknowledgements was a great idea. That way the engineers knew that the data was arriving in the correct way. That was, in computer time, EONS ago.

What about this error checking, and flow control? In UDP how does that happen? Today we have very well written applications that are much better than what we had previously. These apps do a lot of the heavy lifting for us. It would be unusual today to fail to receive a message on your phone, or an email. UDP may be termed as unreliable, but certain applications can take advantage of the way it was built, and real- time apps benefit the most.

Why do you need to know this? Good question. It may help to understand that all of these layers in this big protocol-filled cake are there to help move data from your fingertips to someone's screen halfway across the planet, in just a few clicks and a few micro-seconds. These protocols and traffic moving decisions are made practically instantaneously, and are made based on tons of factors that come from a complex set of devices working together. Layer 4, the Transport layer. It's sort of like the UPS warehouse. Got it. Ok then, Moving on.

LAYER 5: THE SESSION LAYER

The session layer establishes and manages the connections between devices, and when they are done swapping data, the session layer tears down the connection. That sounds super technical; well it's not. If you are old enough to remember using a device called a modem on your computer, then this tale is for you. The modem was a device that used your phone line to connect to another device on "ye olde interweb." Yes, that's right children. This modem would "dial" a number and when the connection was being established, you would hear this terrible electronic noise. It was kind of a Hiss-Hiss-PChing- Krrhing-ching-ching-hiss-hiss. That noise was the Modem making the "Handshake" or connection with the other device. The modems would have to do some very basic stuff during this "Handshake", one being, "Hey what speed is your modem? That's the session layer doing the setup.

Let's relate all this to a simple phone call. You make the call, the other person answers, and you agree to both speak the same language, and take turns speaking. At some point one of you may be droning on a bit much, and may have to ask, "Hey, are you still there?" That part is maintaining the connection. The last part is easy. "Hey, I gotta go, call you later." That is the teardown of the circuit.

The Session Layer is very basic, at least in terms of its responsibility. If you are too young to ever experience using a modem, just try to understand that even the fastest connection to anywhere has to have been set up using some basic rules. I call you, I talk first, I hang up first. Pretty basic. Moving on.

LAYER 6: THE PRESENTATION LAYER

This layer is responsible for helping to organize data that may be in need of further assistance before it is handed off to the Application layer. This layer handles encryption, decryption, and other fun stuff like data formatting and conversion. You yourself, that's right you, have seen this layer in action, when your slightly weird coworker sends you a file to review, and your operating system does not know how to open that file. This layer is the data translator for the network. It deals with file types, and what application will be used to open that file. If your weird buddy is a Linux guy, then he may have sent you a file that will only open in a Linux environment. Go ahead and open an MS WORD document in Notepad and you will see what I mean. The presentation layer is "Presenting" data to the last layer, The Application layer, and it is attempting to ease some of the load by ordering up the correct program to open the file. In order to do just that, it will identify the file type, or the encryption type, so the correct application is then ready to open that file. This takes us to the final layer.

LAYER 7: THE APPLICATION LAYER

This layer provides the interaction between the PC's applications, and the end user; you. This layer provides access to applications such as E-Mail, Messaging, web surfing, and chat services. A few of the Protocols that reside here, include SMTP, TELNET, FTP, TFTP. There are lots more of the same type of protocols at this layer. It is providing some basic services that are very much needed by the user. Some of these protocols have been around for decades.

FTP has been around since the '70s. I call it the Flintstone Transfer Protocol. Yeah, it's that old.

This layer is the only one that allows for user interaction. The user creates an email because there is an interaction here to do that. If the email is then encrypted, that process is being handled at the next stop, which is the Presentation layer. Eventually the email gets put into some semblance of order, addressed with a destination (Layer 4), handed off to a Router (Layer 3), turned into little itty-bitty voltage pulses (Layer 1) and shipped off somewhere. Wow. All within a few micro-seconds too. I don't miss the days of the modem. By the way, the term modem was an acronym for what the darn thing did. It modulated, and then demodulated. Meaning it turned digital signals into analog ones, and then back into digital signals at the other end.

That's enough of this layer business. I would suppose it's possible to learn almost everything that each and every layer does to data and how it does it but for now, let's stick to the basics. There is more to those layers by far, but try to absorb a little of this at a time. Too much intake of the mundane and not critically important stuff can waste the space in your brain that you just might need for the upcoming chapters.

Just a little review.

The OSI model is a way to look at data in its various forms. From bits to bytes, and from packets to segments. It is also there to help digest the somewhat complicated nature of data flow and structures.

Chapter 2

LET'S CRACK THIS EGG. GETTING STARTED WITH EdgeOS

Well, if you are still awake, let's move to getting this thing connected up. Unpack the router, and plug it in. You will need to connect a patch cable to port Eth0 on the router. Do NOT connect to any other Port! You will need to apply a correct address on your local PC to be able to see the router interface. In the Windows Operating System, it's going to be under Network and Sharing in the control panel. You need to navigate to "Change Adapter Settings," over there on the left side of the window. Once in that window, you can right click your Local adapter, select properties, select internet protocol version4. Once you have arrived there you will assign your PC an address that would be in the same network as the default setting on the router. Something like 192.168.1.50. With the subnet of 255.255.255.0. You need not set a default gateway at this time. We will get to that later on. You just cannot use the address 192.168.1.1, as that is the address of the router. Whew. Now you need to open a Browser window, just like you were going to the internet, and you will type in the address 192.168.1.1. The kind folks at Ubiquiti have also designed another way to get into this device that would require you to connect a serial cable to the console port. This cable is often referred to a "Rollover cable". Anyway the cable is a RJ45 to DB9 cable. If your PC does not have a DB9 connection, you would have to get an adapter. Also if your computer is old enough to have a 9 pin serial port, you really should consider buying a NEW ONE. Just saying. Okay, since I started this, I will attempt to finish up. When you make a serial connection to this device, you will need to have some software that will allow you to make this connection. Something like Hyper Terminal. Once the connection is made, (BUY A NEW PC!), inside the Terminal program you would set the Baud Rate to 115200, the Data bits to 8, Parity to none, Stop Bits 1, and Flow

Control to none. This will get you a connection to the command line or CLI of the router.

Okay, let's make a few observations. One, you decided to upgrade your PC, and you donated your old one to one of the seven countries whose name ends in "STAN". You made the web connection to the router and you are faced with a logon screen and then you login with the credentials "ubnt" (no quotation marks) as both the username and password. You agree to the license by selecting a check box, and that's it. You are in. I will be covering security stuff a little later, but you should consider changing the password, to something other than the default of ubnt. This can be done from the Users Tab. Once opened you see the only user at home is that ubnt guy. You might want to create a new user, or just change the ubnt account.

Once you are into the graphical interface, you will want to check the version of the Operating system. This book is based on Firmware Version 1.9.7 + Hotfix4. To get your Router updated, you will need to go to the Ubiquiti website www.UBNT.com and navigate to the downloads section. Once there, go to the EdgeMax section. Find your router in the list on the left side. Once you find your device, select it and you will see the version of Firmware on the right side. Select the newest version and select download. Save that file and remember where you put it. In Windows it will be in the Downloads folder by default. Then, once back in the router, navigate to the System Tab. It's on the bottom. Find the upgrade area, select upgrade and point to the file you just downloaded. It only takes a short time, and one reboot to seal the deal. DO THIS FIRST! Ok, here is a screenshot of the Router. Pay no attention to any of these settings. I just want to get you a little familiar with it.

You see the three pane screen and all of the Tabs across the top, and the two on the bottom.

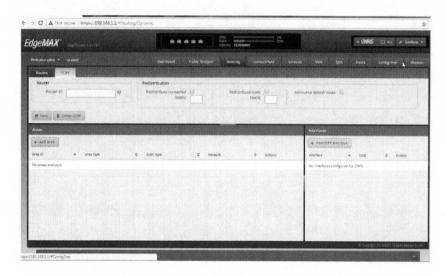

If you upgraded from an older version of the firmware, you will now see many more tabs across the top of the router screen. From left to right they are:

DASHBOARD, kind of an overview of what is connected and will also show the status of connections.

TRAFFIC ANALYSIS, which is designed to show you information about various applications and which device by IP address is using the most bandwidth.

ROUTING, which is where we will create both static and dynamic routes.

FIREWALL/NAT, where we will configure Firewall policies, NAT setup, port forwarding, fun stuff like that.

SERVICES, this is the spot for configuring DNS, DHCP, and PPPOE.

VPN, where you can create two types of VPN connection,

QOS, also known as Quality of Service, where we will be doing some very advanced configuration for setting up Smart Queue, basic queues and advanced Queues. More on these Queues in chapter 6.

Next we have USERS. You were probably here earlier.

CONFIG TREE. I love config tree. It's awesome. This tool gives you the ability to make configuration changes from this utility, rather than from the CLI. Or even better to make adjustments to something that was performed in the CLI. This way if you wanted to change the password for a VPN user, you do not need to trudge back into the CLI. You can make the changes in the Config Tree. I know that some users love to show off their CLI skills. Yay, you're so cool. I personally like this utility because not everyone is a CLI expert. This is a great sort of crossover tool.

The last tab is WIZARDS. Not to worry, we will cover what all these things do and when to use them.

There are two more tabs, and they are down at the bottom. These are SYSTEM, and this is a super critical spot to visit, as it's here that you perform real important tasks like backups and updates.

We have the last one which is Alerts. Here is where you find information about events that the router reports.

Before we go too far, there are a few more things we should check out before starting some basic setup tasks. There are a few items that will always be available no matter what Tab you happen to be at currently. These are:

The Welcome option; if you click here it will allow you to logout of your current Router session.

The CLI button, which we will cover in some detail a little later.

The Tools area; this is for commonly used tools, such as Ping. While down at the bottom we have the Alerts, and the System Tabs that are available under any other chosen tab. Great, now we can begin.

Let's open the System Tab. This Tab will show you the additional settings of Basic Settings. Management Settings, Configuration Management and Device Maintenance. Restart, and Shutdown. The first stop here is the System Host name. This is the name you will give the Router. A little side rant here; my advice is to name your devices in a logical way. What I mean by that is you can name something for the location, or for a connection type. As long as it makes sense to you. I once had a customer name his printer, "Hallway Printer." That would make sense, but in that case, he had three different hallways, each with its own printer.

On the right hand side we have Time Zone. You have two choices here. UTC Time, or Time Zone. If your Network spans many time zones, the best choice is UTC time. This stands for Universal Time Coordinate. It's a formula that Internet devices use to adjust their clocks. On the East Coast of the US, your UTC time is -5, meaning you are five hours behind Greenwich Mean Time. You should set one of these.

The System Gateway Address is just that. This is how your router connects to the Internet. This address is given to you by your service provider.

The Name Server is a DNS server on your local network. If you don't have one, just leave it blank. Domain Name is the name of your Windows Domain, (if you have one). It would look like this. SalesR1.abcinc.com. this would generate a DNS record locally, allowing the device to be "Found" or discovered on the network.

NTP is a time protocol. If you check this box the router will go to the internet to get the correct time. This is pretty important because if your router generates some kind of error or a log file, it's important to know what time it actually occurred.

If you have made any changes, select the Save button down near the bottom on the left side.

In the Next section we have MANAGEMENT SETTINGS. The first one is SSH. This is a secure Protocol used to connect to the router using a program like 'Putty." Putty is a secure program, meaning that is encrypts data going to and from the router. By default it uses port 22. You can change the port for more security if needed. More on how to do security stuff a little later on.

On the other side we have TELNET. This is also a protocol used to access the router but, since it is not secure, I don't recommend using it. It is not selected for that reason.

Back on the left side we have SYSTEM LOG. This is a log file that records things that have happened on the router, and when those events happened. There is a place there to send the log info to a remote server, and there are levels on the pull down menu that would allow you to report different levels of things that went horribly wrong. These levels include, Emergency, Critical, Urgent, Error, Warning, Further Investigation, information, and Debug. Hopefully, someday they will include the popular "Code Brown" alert level. By default the error reporting level is Error. The reason you may want to use this feature is that the router does not have endless room to identify and log silly errors, such as, the router rebooted, or firmware updated.

Next we have UBNT Discovery. This allows the router to be seen using the Discovery tool from Ubiquiti. You should leave this selected.

The last area to configure here is the SMNP Agent. In very plain English, this allows the Router to generate what are called "Agents", that zoom across the Network to a Server that would collect and Organize these "Agents" into a form that the Network admin can see and act upon if needed. Now this is disabled by default, and requires the configuration of an application running on a local sever to collect these agents and alert the appropriate person. The current version of this is V1, and it may not be compatible with some versions of the Collection software that your admin may be using, so a little research may be required.

Next we have the Configuration Management and Device Maintenance area. The controls in this section manage configuration of the device. Here you can upgrade the Firmware, or reset the Router to factory defaults.

The first area to use would be the BACK UP CONFIG. It is very important that you have a copy of your configuration BEFORE bad things happen. So click the DOWNLOAD BACKUP CONFIG File. A little bit of advice. It is good practice to keep your backups in a secure location. Although User login passwords are encrypted, other important things are not encrypted. Like passwords for VPN's.

Moving right along we have the UPLOAD CONFIG FILE. This is used to take a configuration file that you may have backed up prior, and restore it. Above all else, keep recent backups. Before uploading a backup, make a new one. Just to be on the safe side.

UPGRADE SYSTEM IMAGE. This is something you're going to need to do. Hopefully, you have already downloaded the correct, and most current system image and you put it where you can find it. You should have also made a backup (if needed). Select UPLOAD SYSTEM IMAGE, and UPLOAD A FILE, and browse for the file you downloaded, then select CHOOSE. The router will count its fingers and toes, do a proper reboot, and then the new firmware will be in place.

Another short note; if you lose power, or kick out the power cord of the router during this process, you may damage the router. I once did this to a Windows PC to see if they were kidding when they told me this. Turns out they were not kidding. My BIOS upgrade failed, and I was the proud new owner of a large paperweight.

Next we have the RESET CONFIG TO DEFAULT. Guess what that does? As always you may want to back up your current configuration before you do this.

RESTART AND SHUT DOWN ROUTER. Rather than just unplugging and then plugging the router back in, use this feature.

Okay, so now you have a router. It has the latest firmware loaded on it. It has the correct stuff, like time zone. Now let's do some damage.

I like to start at the USERS Tab. Making a new user is a good idea. The new user, can be a full-fledged administrator, or just have an Operator account. An operator cannot make permanent changes to the router itself. It's sort of a like creating a Read Only user. Of course, you want to make yourself a user account. Do it. Give yourself a very complex password; it's the way to go.

Here's a short note on passwords. Long ago my father told me, "Locks tend to keep honest people honest." He meant that a padlocked tool shed is most likely able to keep out people who should not be there, unless that person steals tools for a living. For this special group, we need better locks. I always recommend a complex password. There are four elements that can be part of a password: uppercase letters, lowercase letters, symbols, like the $ sign, and numbers. I say try to use all of them. It will make it very difficult for someone to break into your router.

Also at the User tab we have information that shows how many connections a user may have open, the duration of that connection, and when that user connected, sorted by date. Remember I told you earlier that setting the time and date on a router is very important? Here is one of the places where that become important.

A note here on the Administrator or the ubnt account. It's a good idea to have actual accounts that relate to actual living persons. Otherwise you might have logs that only show that the ubnt user was logged in when something went off the rails.

Here in the land of Users you will also find a tab marked REMOTE. These are users that are using the router remotely. They may be using a PPTP VPN. They might be using PPPOE, or L2TP to access the router. There is a table that displays information about the user logged in to the router. The table displays the Name of the user, the type of connection they have made, and the duration of that connection. You also can click on a column to sort the information. Don't be shy, click away. Ok Stop.

Let's go back to the Main Screen also known as the Dashboard. This Tab will show you three other screens, and this is the place that you will start. On the left side you will see SERVICES. This area will give you an overview of routing; route type, NAT status, Firewall status, along with the number of firewall rules, and DHCP Server status. I will cover all of these items a little later in greater detail. Let's kill more trees.

On the Bottom part of the screen you see Interfaces. You have the option of displaying them by type, such as Ethernet, or you can select the ALL tab to do just that. The first interface listed is ETH0. It shows the IP address, the MTU, the TX and the RX rate, and whether that port is connected or disconnected.

To the far right you see an ACTION tab; select it. Once here you can assign the interface an IPv4 address, and IPv6 address. You can have this interface receive an address from a DHCP server. You can assign a static IP address here. If you want to have the same IP address all the time, then assign a static address here. Let's break a few things down.

You need several things configured on the router to allow your computer access to the Internet. First off, you need to have a valid IP address on the LAN side of the router. That's the side your PC is on. You also need to have an address on the WAN side of the router. This is an address assigned to you by your service provider, so first things first, you have a line coming in from your service provider. It may be in the form of a Modem, or large ugly device that has a label on it like LAN, or WAN. If you see the big ugly thing, then plug a cable into the port labeled LAN, and the other end into a port on your Router. Let's just say you use Eth2. Then if your Modem, or big ugly device, is working correctly it would assign an address to Port Eth2 on your router. Inside the interface screen you would select DHCP. This would ensure you are getting an assigned address on that port. Now you have a WAN address.

Next you need a LAN address. You assign another port on the Router to the LAN side, let's say Eth1. You can assign an address and subnet of your choosing. If you need more training on IP addressing, please fast forward to the next chapter: IP Addressing and Subnets. Go ahead and review that and I will meet you back here.

Hey your back. Good. Let's go ahead and assign the IP address. We'll make it a static address and assign it to your Eth1. For our use we will use 192.168.2.1/24. Now select the ACTION TAB down at the end of Eth1, and from there you can assign the address.

You have other items here you can select as well. You can select the MTU, this stands for Maximum Transmission Unit, and the default value is 1500. You can leave it be. You also have a checkbox for Proxy Arp. I have put several pages of definitions in the back of the book, so this is one you should look up. You could also put in a description here as well. Okay, so you have a LAN address, the router is receiving an address from the ugly Modem, and we have a few other items to check off our list for you to be connected to the Internet.

You have to setup DNS. DNS is a service, and you will find it at the Tab labeled SERVICES. Here you will set the interface for DNS forwarding. The EdgeRouter does not perform DNS, but forwards those requests to a DNS

Server. So what is the mystery of DNS? Here is how this service works. Every website that you visit in your daily lap around the Web is actually an IP address. For example, if you were checking your high school buddy out on Facebook, you would just type www.facebook.com. But the page you are visiting is actually at 31.13.70.36. That is an IP address. The DNS service merely converts the name that you entered, (www.facebook.com) into an IP address. You see, the problem here is us; humans. We are not very good at remembering a set of numbers, but we can easily remember the web address as Facebook. Your computers see the address as an IP address, so DNS does the conversion for us. Heck, I go into the kitchen and forget why I was going there in the first place, or I look for my glasses that are currently on top of my head, so how am I going to remember 4 groups of numbers? Well I don't have to because DNS does the heavy lifting for me, so we need to tell our router what interfaces to listen for DNS requests. These listening interfaces are on the LAN side. The request is going to be forwarded to a device on the internet that does this conversion all the time. The DNS server that many people use is the Google DNS server residing at 8.8.8.8.

Also on the SERVICE TAB for DNS you will see the entry for Cache size. This refers to the number of Cached lookups. For instance, if you set the number at 100, the router will keep the first 100 web address to IP address connections or mappings, right there in memory, so it does not have to forward the request to a Internet Service Provider (ISP), or that service at 8.8.8.8. In other words it's much faster to have the address in Cache.

There is another entry here as well, and that is ADD LISTEN INTERFACE. If you have more than one LAN, and it connects on another Ethernet interface, then just hit the dropdown arrow and add the interface. You can always remove an interface here as well.

Now you have a LAN interface setup, a WAN interface, and DNS. You need just a little more work to get connected. Let's go back and think about addresses. The devices connected to your LAN side of the router. Let's say the physical wire runs from the LAN port, (192.168.2.1) down to a switch. This switch is the place that you will plug in your PC, and maybe a Wireless Access point (WAP), or a camera, or a gaming console or even a television. All these devices need an IP address to function properly. There are two ways that this can happen. You can manually assign these devices an address, subnet mask, default gateway, and DNS of your choice, or you can use the DHCP service to do that for you.

The DHCP service resides at the SERVICES Tab. Here you will set up your first DHCP Pool. Okay, so the first thing you want to do is set up the DHCP Server. Select ADD DHCP SERVER. Feel free to give it a snappy name. You will note that when you see the little star thingy next to something, it means this must be filled in so a DHCP SERVER NAME is required. I call mine TESTLAB.

Under that you must fill in the SUBNET. Now remember our router interface connecting our LAN segment was 192.168.2.1. You need to put the Network address here and the subnet in Slash notation. Like 192.168.2.0/24. Next you will select the start of the RANGE of numbers being allocated so I have 192.168.2.2, and the RANGE STOP I have is 192.168.1.254. This way I am having the DHCP server hand out every possible address in this Network.

Next you will enter the ROUTER address; use 192.168.2.1. Next put in the address of the Primary DNS server. You can get this from your provider, or you can just go with 8.8.8.8. There is also one labeled DNS 2. This is called the Secondary DNS server. You can use the providers address here or you can use another public DNS server like 8.8.4.4.

DHCP is a service. It can run as a service on a router or on a separate actual server. It's also a standard service, so it can run on a MS Windows based Server, a UNIX Server, or a LINUX server, it doesn't really matter. What does matter is what it does. When a PC (CLIENT) does not have an IP address, the device will broadcast for this service. The broadcast is heard by a DHCP server, who then offers an address to the client. Once they agree on an address, the address is given to the client, and the DHCP Server then notifies the DNS server of the new Client IP to Client Name mapping. Everyone is happy. Not only does it hand the client an IP address, it also gives out the proper subnet mask, and default gateway information, along with the correct DNS Server to forward it's DNS requests. Moving on.

If you are connected to the switch that, in turn is connected to the router, your PC will be obtaining an address from the DHCP Service. We are nearly ready to get online with that PC. We have to complete one more task. We have a LAN address. We have a WAN address. We have configured the DNS Service to LISTEN on one of our LAN ports. Now we need to go back to the router interface and go to the FIREWALL/NAT tab. We need to set up NAT. First off, a quick NAT reference.

NAT stands for Network Address Translation. What it does it very important. It allows a connection from your PRIVATE NETWORK ADDRESS, to roam around on the 'inter-webs' by temporarily assigning you a PUBLIC ADDRESS. It can use the public address of the router to let you out, so to speak. Private addresses cannot be used for the internet, so we need NAT to convert our LAN addresses, also known as a SOURCE ADDRESS, to one we can use. The usual way to do this is by opening the NAT tab under the FIREWALL/NAT tab. Here you will select the NAT rule to use. You want to use a Source NAT Rule because you are changing the Source address from that of your PC to that of the router's public address.

Select Add Source Nat Rule and give it a name, then choose Config. This will open a new window. Do NOT worry, I know there are tons of choices here, but we will not need to worry about them all right now. You will only select a few things for the NAT rule to allow your packets to move out of your LAN and onto to the WAN. You do not need to enter a description here but you can if you want. You want to make sure that the ENABLE box is selected. You need to select the OUTBOUND Interface. That is the connection to the WAN, or the big ugly Modem thing. If that cable is on Eth0, then select that interface from the dropdown box. You will select MASQUERADE as the Translation type. This assigns the correct address and a Random Port number to the session that you are having online.

Each online session will use a separate port number to identify where the packets should be sent. Masquerade is also called Port Address Translation, or PAT. You do not need to select anything else. Click the SAVE button on the bottom.

One big thing is next. It's the purpose for the book; routing. To get somewhere, actually to get anywhere, we need a route to follow. In our case, we have the LAN, WAN, DNS, DHCP, NAT stuff all done so we are practically there. Your router will create a route to the internet for you. You see, it understands what your LAN addresses are, and it understands the WAN part as well, and you just told it, "Hey, I want to use the WAN address as my source address, instead of the LAN address."

That was NAT and routing is the last step to getting online. Yet there is another feature that you may want to include prior to getting online; the Firewall feature. The Firewall is a complex group of checkboxes and rules, and therefore it has its very own chapter. That's down there in Chapter 5 and you just might want to read all that stuff prior to getting online. It would be a good idea. Now, if you just wanted to test out your connections, and you do not have a PC connected up, you can open the TOOLS icon, select PING and ping the address of a public DNS server, like 8.8.8.8, to see if you have connectivity. By the way, PING is a utility, as is Trace Route. Both of these tools operate under the Protocol ICMP. Internet Control Messaging Protocol. PING stands for "Packet Internet Groper." Yup, Groper. Sounds like the Muppet who never really worked out. Anyway, this is the tool to use to see if you are moving packets across the Web, or your local Network. It was named after the sound that sonar makes, since it acts like sonar on a network, identifying where something is by measuring distance and speed.

WIZARDS, AND WHY WE LIKE THEM

You may have noticed that there is a TAB all the way on the right that says Wizards. When you open it, you will find that there are several wizards listed. Some of them are Setup Wizards, and some are Feature Wizards. The Setup Wizards, are very cool and very easy to understand. There is the "Basic Setup" wizard setting up the router as a SOHO (Small Office, Home Office) router. The Basic Setup Wizard will guide you through the setup of a typical small office setup. It configures the LAN and the WAN Ports for you. It sets up your NAT masquerade for you too. It does something else that's awesome, and that is setting up a default Firewall for you. Yeah, it also does the DNS forwarding. It will allow you to configure User accounts, and it will do TCP MSS clamping for a PPPoE connection. TCP MSS Clamping sounds painful, but go and look it up if you feel the need. Now that you did the Google search and are still not sure what it is, here is a quick once-over.

Certain types of traffic, such as VPN traffic, are basically hiding some of their information. Some of the stuff that is in the header of a packet is hidden. Well, when you do that, the packet looks like it's no longer the correct size. The standard Ethernet chunk is 1500 bytes, and some connection types are changing that. Now this would not be a problem normally as we are also sending a control message that would explain this to downstream devices. But due to security firewalls that are beyond your control, these control messages may become dropped. So we implement clamping to let everyone know that this is the size packet we want. This book is focusing on the entry level routing, and I will probably have a much longer and exceedingly complex explanation in higher lever texts.

There are two wizards that will let you set up the LAN to WAN stuff. One of them will allow you to set up two LANs. It's kind of nice if you want a test environment. By the way, the Basic Setup Wizard is the same as the LAN to WAN2 Wizard.

You will also see two Load Balancing Wizards. One of them is a basic setup that will allow you to have two internet connections and should one of them fail, the other will take charge. There is a second Failover wizard that does a secondary setup using wireless links and that is beyond the scope of this book. (Way, way Beyond)

There are several Feature Wizards as well. They are also beyond the scope of this text, but let's talk about them very briefly. I did mention the TCP MSS Clamping, that's used to set up traffic in VPNs and it keeps the packets accounted for and remaining the correct size.

The DNS wizard is used for larger naming structures. It will be used in a Windows Domain environment for instance.

The UPnP, now that's a unique one. It stands for Universal Plug and Play and it's for hardware that understands the UPnP stuff like gamers and game consoles. These are devices that use UPnP and I can pretty much guarantee that you would rather use this little wizard over having to set up port forwarding for someone playing some role-playing game.

The last one here is the VPN status wizard. It keeps an eye on any existing VPN connections to make sure they are working and still secure.

I did not go into a few of the Tabs, as they are beyond what we are trying to do in this text, but I will give a brief, Reader Digest, version of what they do.

TRAFFIC ANALYSIS. I briefly mentioned before that this tab looks at the traffic going to the EdgeRouter. It can look at the traffic from the clients as well. It can be helpful when it comes to looking at high usage clients, or what type of traffic it is that might cause you some headaches. In later versions we have the ability to do what is noted as DPI, or Deep Packet Inspection. It's this DPI that allows us to see what application clients are using to move the highest amount of data.

The last one I want to mention is the CONFIG TREE. It's a wonderful tool. It is the crossover between the Command line and the Graphical interface we call the GUI. Or GOOEY.

I like the GUI. I like to get into the router, get my stuff set up, and get out. For me it's like buying underwear at Walmart; I'm in and out in minutes. Now someone might tell you that it can all be done through the CLI. Yes it can, but I would rather make three or five clicks of the mouse and be done with it. My typing skills are not great, and my memory is even worse, so looking up the correct command and the correct way to enter it takes time and practice. With that being said I want to give you a brief primer on using the CLI. And here is some basic navigation for now.

THE CLI

The CLI, or the Command Line Interface, is accessed either through a program such as Putty, or from the GUI where there is a Box in the upper right part of the screen next to the Tools menu. This CLI box will be available no matter what other sub tab that you may select.

So why don't I just use the Graphical Interface for my entire configuration? Well the short answer is you may not be able to use every option in the GUI, and the CLI will let you get very granular on some commands. Later on there is a VPN section and you will be using the CLI to configure the VPN, as some of the settings we use for our example are not available in the GUI. For beginners let's walk through this just to get familiar. Once you select the CLI box, or log onto the CLI through Putty, you will have to Authenticate. This will happen even if you are currently logged onto the GUI. The first part of the Command Line will show the User who is logged in, and the second part shows the name of the router. And at the end of the username Routername string you see a $ sign.

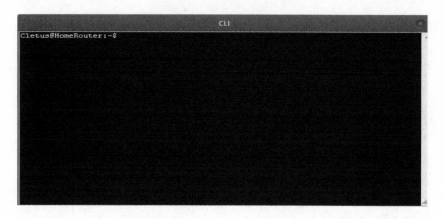

```
Cletus@HomeRouter:~$
```

That $ sign indicates what is called **Operational Mode**. This mode will allow you to take a gander at the current state of the Router, and you can run some commands here. The other Mode is called **Configuration Mode**. And this mode will allow you to make changes that can be written to what is called the Configuration File, and that's the file that the Router reads when it boots up to see what settings to apply. You cannot make changes that will still be there after a reboot when in Operational mode. Another important note here is that on the EdgeOS you have the ability to create users that are either Operators, or Admins. And if you make a user an Operator, they will not be able to enter Configuration Mode.

Ok, separate from the Modes, we have what are called Configuration States. There are three:

Working: If you are in the CLI, and you are configuring something, let's say you are setting up a Bridge interface; you are in the Working State. That means that you have yet to apply any of the changes you have made.

Active: This becomes the current state after you have committed any of the changes that you have made. However these changes will not remain if you reboot the Router. To tell the Router to update the Boot File, you will need to enter the command SAVE.

Boot: This mode represents what the Router will load when it is rebooted.

Now then, whether it is a small change or something more complex, you have to enter the Commit command. Now if you enter this command you will also have to confirm that change. To avoid the "Are you sure?" portion, you can use the commit-confirm command. Now if you happen to walk away from the Router for more than 5 minutes before entering the confirm portion of the command, the Router will return to its previous configuration.

USEFUL TIPS

The EdgeOS CLI has a few features that will make things a little easier for you.

TAB Key. Hitting the TAB key will complete the command that you are typing. And it will also show you the possible completions as well.

Here are the results of typing show in and then hitting the tab key.

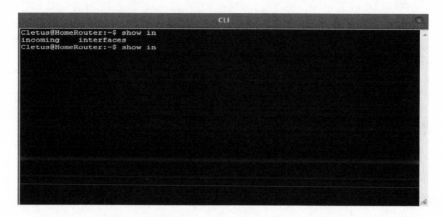

```
Cletus@HomeRouter:~$ show in
incoming    interfaces
Cletus@HomeRouter:~$ show in
```

It will show both possible completions. If you were to type show inter... and then the tab, you have typed enough letters to allow the OS to understand the only possible completion would be the word interfaces. I am not a great typist, and I love this feature.

- The Question mark. Hitting the ? will also show you possible completions.

- Configure command allows you to leave operational mode and enter Configuration Mode.

- The Exit command will allow you leave a Mode or terminate the CLI session.

If you are typing a series of command entries, and you change your mind you can type exit discard, to discard your previous entries.

Context sensitive help. This means that hitting the Tab or the question mark will allow the system to try to help you. If you type a partial word then the Tab, you will see the possible endings. If you have typed one word of the command and then a space and then Tab, you will see what word or function would be the next thing to enter.

Ok, here are a few basic commands that you might need to know.

OPERATIONAL COMMANDS

`configure`: This takes you to Configure Mode, but only if you are an Admin

`reboot`: Will cause the Router to reboot, but only after a confirmation

`show arp`: Displays arp neighbors

`show ip route`: Displays current Routing Table

`show conntrack`: Displays Connections in a table. Sort of like Netstat

CONFIGURATION MODE COMMANDS

`commit`: Apply changes to the Active Configuration

`commit-confirm`: Apply those same changes but will require you to confirm before a countdown timer expires

`Delete`: Delete part of a configuration

`edit firewall`: Allows you to make insertion based edits

`edit services`: Move to a line in the configuration file to mak edits

`exit`: Leave configuration Mode

`save`: Save everything to the boot configuration

`set`: Add changes to the configuration

`set interfaces`: Create, modify or delete interfaces. These interfaces include Ethernet, Bridge, Loopback and tunnel

`set system`: Host name, gateway-address – lots of options here

You will do more work at the command line in the VPN chapter.

Backups. I cannot stress this point enough. You should always maintain a backup copy of your routers configuration. Be the Boy Scout. Please be prepared, bad things can happen.

The Config Tree is the place where I can do some things that simply cannot be done in the GUI, but are a little more intuitive to perform. One way I like to use this utility is to edit some parameters. If you already have set up a Traffic control policy, you can get into this utility and make some changes. You would notice that anything you have already configured will be in bold, and it makes it rather simple to work your way through the configurations. We will be looking at this a little later when we set up a VPN. For now, we can move on to more excitement with the care and feeding of IP addressing.

Chapter 3

IP ADDRESSING AND SUBNET MASKING

Ok, if you came here to quickly learn about IP addressing. I am sorry. This will not be so quick. Have some coffee, put your feet up and just let it happen. For those out there who already know plenty about IPv4 and subnets feel free to skip ahead and come back when needed to refresh your memory.

What makes IP addressing unique? Let's start at the beginning. All computers that are part of a Routed Network, are required to have a few items that make them work correctly on this Network. Firstly, each PC or device such as an IPAD or a tablet or a phone, even a printer, require a **VALID IP** address. Each device will need the correct **Subnet Mask** setting, and the correct **Default Gateway** address.

Let's go with that. A valid address sounds easy. It would be an address that is not duplicated on the Network. So let's break it down in smaller bits to help this go down easier.

If you are on a Windows machine, just open the search programs and files window, type the letters cmd, then hit enter. This takes you to the command line. A black and white screen. At the command line, type the command Ipconfig. Just that one word, and hit enter. Next to the line IPv4 you should see something like 192.168.1.19. Or you may see 10.1.1.2. Fear not, that number is your IP address. You will also see the Subnet Mask here, which is probably 255.255.255.0. And you will see a Gateway address as well. Probably 192.168.1.1. Ok, don't panic if those are not the exact numbers. Ok, now I know most beginners have no idea what these numbers are, or why they are Important. Hang in there.

Remember I mentioned that the PC will need a VALID IP address? That is because without a valid address, the connection to other devices, including the Router will fail. Let's look at the Anatomy of an address.

An IPv4 address is 32 bits long. And those bits are divided into what are called Octets. There are 4 Octets in the address. The first thing to remember is that you will see the address written down or shown as something like **192.168.1.2**. You see those dots, those periods between each set of numbers? There are 4 sets of numbers total. Now the PC, or your other IPv4 devices don't really see the numbers the same way we do. Again, we are Humans, and as such we have a good grasp on numbers systems like base 10. Most people being born with 10 digits have an easier time counting this way. So our numbering system is Base 10. Meaning we use a digital type readout, like a digital clock. Right, well the computers of the world will display these number types for our convenience, but they see the number 192 in binary, which looks like 1100000. The system that the computer uses is Base 2. Binary math here we come! Ok I am going to try to keep it simple. In each of our Octets, we have 8 digits. Each position has an actual value. These numbers and values remain constant in each Octet. The VALUE of the far left digit is 128. And as we go from left to right, the value will drop in Half. Like this. 128,64,32,16,8,4,2,1. There are the 8 digits. So how did 192 become 11000000? Well add the first two digits together. 128+64=192. Where there are 1's in the Octet, that indicates that the value is ON, or TRUE. So the first two values are on. Therefore we just add them up. So let's do a little Binary to decimal conversion.

Decimal 1= Binary 1(The farthest digit on the right is ON!) It can look like this, 00000001. Or we can just leave out the 0's for now.

Decimal 2= Binary 10, (The second to the last number is ON)

Decimal 3= Binary 11, (Both of the last 2 are ON, Therefore 2+1=3)

Decimal 4= Binary 100, (The value of the third to last digit is 4)

Decimal 5=Binary 101, (The value of the third to the last digit and the last digit added together.)

Decimal 6=Binary 110, (The 4 value and the two are a 1, so they are added up)

Ok, I think that should do it. Just try to remember we start from left to right, and use 128 as the far left hand number. The values drop in half as we move from left to right. If we went the other way, and looked at right to left, the first Value is 1, and as we move to the left the value doubles. Now again each of the four octet do this the same way. So there is no new math here.

192=11000000. The next octet is 168. So That a little harder. 10101000. Ok, add the values up. We have the first one of 128, then we skip 64, (it's a 0) the next value is 32, we skip 16, the last value with a 1, or TRUE is 8. So 128+16+8=168.

So there is the basic math that the PC's and routers of the world see. It's the same numbers, but they are just expressed differently. Let's try some binary math out.

Binary 1=Decimal 1.

Binary 10=Decimal value of 2. Remember the octet contains 8 digits. So when I write Binary 10, I am leaving out the leading 0's. Otherwise it would look like 00000010. That's Binary 10, or decimal value of 2. Since the one "True" or "ON bit" is in the position of the value of 2. Remember, starting from right to left, its 1, then doubled each time we move to the left.

Hang in there. How about a Binary value of 1011? Starting from the right we have an on value for the number 1, the number 2, we have off for the number 4, and an "On" value for the number 8. Remember we are doubling the numbers as we move left, and halving the numbers as we move to the right. So if you got the decimal answer of 11, then you are catching on. Go ahead, get a cookie. I'll wait.

Now just to make sure that you understand the conversion of these numbers, in Windows, press the Windows key with one finger and punch the letter "r" with a spare finger. You will see the run command. Type the letters "calc" and hit the enter key. You have opened the calculator. Under the view tab at the top select "Programmer". Now key in the number 192, and on the left hand side you will see a box that already has selected dec, so check the button next to bin and you will see the converted number. Spend a little time here and put in the octets of the address that you saw when you ran ipconfig. Take your time. Cool huh.

So I want to go and back up just a little, and go back to what I mentioned before about the IP address of a device and how it has to be a VALID one. Well that must mean that some addresses are not valid. That is correct. Some addresses are used for different purposes. Let break these up into a few groups.

A long time ago, in this galaxy, Internet Engineers decided that every device that connected to the vast spider web of interconnected devices, should have a Unique name. Like Server1, or PC12. Or Phred. Something like that. And since the Number of devices on this web were limited, it became the way things were. Every Device had a unique name. It was called a HOST. And a Host file was a file that had a mapping of that name, to a unique IP address. Wow! So if you were on the early web, every so often you would download a list of new host names and it would show you the associated IP address of that device. Well now we still have Host names for our PC's and our servers, but since there are so many these days on the internet, we don't find, or connect, or message each other based on a host name. We connect to a Web Site, or to a Device holding the programming for a website, based on IP addresses. Right now, as I write this, we have over 660 million web sites. To long of a list to keep on our local PC's would not be possible or practical.

So these same engineers decided to break up the Internet by addresses. They decided on what they called Class A, B, C, D, and E. The idea was brilliant.

Large Business entities would have an Address that would match up with the size of that entity. So a huge company would be given a class A address. Here is how the classes actually broke down.

When reading the first Octet only, The Class A addresses went from 1-126

So it would look something like 19.1.1.1 , This is a Class A address. The first octet (19) being between 1 and 126. Let's cover some basic rules. There are Two addresses in the Class A that are not used for the Devices on the internet. The first is the Address that starts with 10. Any address that starts with 10 cannot be used on the Internet, as the 10 designates what is called a "Private address. "The other Class A address that is not used, was designated as a Testing address. Also called a Loopback address. That address is 127.0.0.1. I know that you are thinking that 127 is not a Class A address, but it is. I just made the range 1-126 , due to this address being used for testing. So let's look at the ranges.

Class A. 1-126 (127) 1.0.0.1 to 126.255.255.254

Class B. (128-191) 128.1.0.1 to 191.255.255.254

Class C. (192-223) 192.0.1.1 to 223.255.254.254

Class D. (224-240) 224.0.0.0 to 239.255.255.255

Class E. (Experimental, or Reserved for future use) (241-254.) 240.00.0 to 254.255.255.254

Okay, now the next part of this is trying to understanding the subnet mask.

If we go back and look at the way it was originally designed, we would see something like this. Let's take a Class A address of 25.1.1.1 We would see a Subnet mask of 255.0.0.0 This was always the case of a Class A address. The Mask would never change.

WHAT IS THE SUBNET MASK?

That is a great question. A subnet mask is a number that basically tells the Device, The PC the Laptop, the Server, Which "Network " that the device is connected to, or is a participant in. In this setup the "Mask" separates the Network Portion of the address from the Host Portion. Now I know this is getting a little complex, bear with me, you will be fine. In the original setup of our Class A address, the first Octet of the address, represented the network. In other words, our 25.1.1.1 address has the mask of 255.0.0.0, so the mask is covering our first octet only, so therefore our first octet is the Network portion. Our network is 25. The other numbers will belong to our devices on that 25 Network.

In essence, Class A addresses always had the Subnet Mask of 255.0.0.0 or Net.node.node.node. Where the number 25 is the "Net" and the rest of the address will be assigned to devices, or "Nodes".

Class B networks used the First Two octets to describe the Network, and the last two octets to describe the Host portion. Like this Class B. Net.Net.Node.Node. So a Class B address of 182.190.1.10, the 182.190 is the actual Network, and the portion of 1.10 represents the host portion.

Class C Networks looking like 198.199.10.1. Would have the Mask 255.255.255.0.

Or , Net.Net.Net.Node. The First three octets describe the Network, and the very last Octet describes the Host portion. So that represented what came to be called as "Classful" addressing. It was all so organized. You had large companies using Class A addresses, and small companies using the smaller Class C addresses. Returning to what I mean as a valid address, we need to further review addresses that are used as "Private IP addresses." These again are addresses that are being used inside the Local Area Network (LAN), and are not used for any public facing devices. There are three sets of these Private IP addresses.

Class A. 10. Anything. Yup. 10 .1.1.1 all the way up to 10.255.255.254.

Class B. 172.16.0.0 all the way up to 172.168.31.255 Class C. 19.168.Anything. Such as 192.168.1.200.

If you have ever looked at the device given to you by your service provider, (Comcast, Time Warner) they will be using one of the Private addresses for your LAN. Alright, got that? No, if we fast forward a little bit, the numbers folks realized that we would still run out of addresses. Who knew that everyone would be using so many devices that could interconnect? So along came what would be known as "Classless" Addressing. In this addressing scenario we are no longer limited to having just 8 bits for a Subnet Mask in a Class A address. In fact the Mask could be using many more digits, like this.

12.1.1.1

255.255.0.0

So what is our Network Portion? Well it's the first 2 Octets. 12.1. That's the Network. What is the Host Portion? That would be the last two octets. 1.1

Now using Classless numbering gave us many more numbers, or Network/Host combinations. Furthering the use of the IPV4 system.

So hopefully by this time we have a better idea about what a VALID IP address is composed of. An address that has not been duplicated elsewhere on the LAN, and an address that meets the requirements of our Network. A local area Network is comprised of addresses in the Private range. Web Servers that we connect to on the internet are represented by a Public IP address. One that is not only public but is also associated with the name of the Website as well. The HOST name. So WWW.Google.com has a Public IP address. It actually has several. Hey, it's a big internet out there. The SUBNET MASK is a feature of the LAN addresses, as it informs the local hosts as to the Network they reside upon, (NETWORK ID) and the range of addresses within their range. So in other words, other devices that they can communicate with directly. It also identifies the BROADCAST ADDRESS of that particular LAN so devices know where to send a Broadcast.

Let me translate this craziness into a short story. The LAN can be thought of as similar to a large apartment building. All of the residents live at the same Address of 12 Main Street. If one of those residents wanted to send a message to another person at the same APT building, they could just slip it under the neighbors door. If they did not know the whereabouts of the neighbors APT, they could send a Broadcast. "HEY, HARRY. WHATS YOUR APARTMENT NUMBER?" Maybe using a bullhorn. You see, modern computers know their neighbors because of the Subnet Mask. So if I needed to send a message, I just need to know the right place to slip the note under the correct door. All of the devices on a particular network know the "Broadcast Address." They all have Bullhorns. When they want to find one another, that's the way they do it. Oh, and that APT number? It is represented by a port on our local switch. The last part of this story is why we have a Default Gateway. In our APT Building scenario, the default gateway would be the front door. The way we all get out. When our message is addressed to somebody on the internet, and not someone who is on our LAN. Our devices will send the message to the gateway, where it will be forwarded to our Friendly Internet Service Provider. He will then send it off to the correct destination. I often tell my students it is far more important to understand these basic building blocks such as IP addressing. I will have them use an online IP calculator, for those times when they need to use a custom mask length. If they are creating VLANS or they need to address more clients or hosts, and using the online calculator can show them that option.

SMALL LAB

Do it! Navigate to the Website http://www.subnet-calculator.com.

Now once you are there you will see a lovely blue screen and on the top left area you will see the area labeled Network Class. You also see A B, or C. So select the Network class of C. It's a round(Radio) button. You will see the address of 192.168.0.1, and under that you see the Mask of 255.255.255.0 using 0 bits of masking. That just means it is using the default mask. And right under that you see how many "Networks" this mask gives you. Just one. One the right side we see Mask bits, and Hosts per Network. Don't worry about the other three things above. For our demonstration we don't care. Mask bits shows 24. That is how many binary digits long the Subnet Mask is. 24 bits long. This setup of numbers will produce for you 254 VALID IP ADDRESSES! Under this we see the entire range of the actual numbers. 192.168.0.1 All the way up to 192.168.0.254. The last two fields show the Network ID and the Broadcast address. These two individual addresses are not valid for client PC; s. The first is the Network ID. Hey that's 12 Main Street. That the address of our LAN. So if it's the address of the LAN, it can't be used to address a printer, or a PC. The last individual number is the Broadcast address. And that's the address that all of our devices on the

Network send out their broadcasts. So that number also cannot be applied to an actual PC.

So let's change a few numbers around. For now leave the IP address alone, but change the length of the mask. Make it 255.255.255.128. How many clients do we get with that Mask? How many Subnets? 2? That's right we now get two subnets. We can see that the first Range is 192.168.0.1 up to 192.168.0.126. So our address of 192.168.0.1 is in the first network. So let's change the IP address at the top of the screen to 192.168.0.130. You can see that this IP address is in the second "Network". This one is going from 192.168.0.129 up to 192.168.0.254. This means that the Broadcast address will also be different from the first group. So can a PC with the address of 192.168.0.1 and a Mask of 255.255.255.128 send a direct message to a PC with the address of 192.168.0.130 and the same length Mask? I hope you said "NO!" They are on two separate networks. So one Network is at 12 Main Street. And the other is at 15 Main Street. They are two separate things. To be able to communicate between these two devices on two separate networks would require a Router.

This Calculator is really easy to use, and it's also fun. Try another.

Let's say that you wanted a LAN large enough to accommodate 450 computers. You want them all to be on the same LAN. To have all of these devices able to see all the other devices. So they would share the same Network ID, and the same Broadcast ID as well. Change the Network to a "B". Yup. Now you will the numbers that Autofill change. Well we want our old numbers back. So delete the number that they give you. The 172 whatever number, and type in

192.168.0.1. Now on the Right Hand side select the dropdown arrow next to Host Per Subnet. We wanted 450, but that number does not appear. So the best we can do is 510, since we know that 254 is not enough. So, we get 510 VALID HOST IP ADDRESSES!

I Know I should not Yell like that but.... Do you see what the length of the Mask is? Its 23 bits long. One less than before. But due to the way Binary numbers work, it's giving us one more exponent to use for our Host PCs and one less for our Network. In fact if you were to change the Mask to 22 bits long (255.255.252.0.) we get 1022 hosts. Fool around with the calculator for a bit. You can change the Networks or the Hosts, or a combination of these.

Let's now go back to our Example. 450 IP addresses on the same Network.

Our Network ID is 192.168.0.0. Our Broadcast address is 192.168.1.255. The range of IP addresses is 192.168.0.1 to 192.168.1.254. The new Subnet Mask is 255.255.254.0

Remember before I had mentioned about Private Addressing. We had the ability to use any of these numbers for our LAN. In fact in the calculator you can get the correct results using a Class A number of 10.Anything. Try it. Select Network Class, "A", leave the 10 number in there and just change the dropdown box next to Hosts per Subnet. Change it to give us the 510 number. Just like before. Now you will see that the Mask length does not change, just the LAN addressing.

Ok I want to clean a few things up. First off I am sure there are literally hundreds of IP Subnet Calculators that you can find on the Web. It matters not to me which one or ones you prefer. I am in no way affiliated with the website http://www.subnet-calculator.com, nor am I being paid to mention them. Meh. Use what you are comfy with. Secondly, I don't want the reader to fret over that feeling that they are overwhelmed by all that Masking, and addressing. If you are starting out in this field it will soon become a part of your everyday life, and rightly so, you will begin to get a little more comfortable with it. I would like to review a few important points about this chapter.

1. All devices that are part of a "Routed Network" must have a Valid IP, Subnet Mask, and a Gateway. You will need DNS information as well, but we will get to that in depth a little later.

2. There are "Private IP's", and there are Public Ones. Know the difference.

3. Computers and related devices see numbers in Binary, not Decimal Notation.

4. Use the calculators. Make sure that you have the correct information, before you begin to assign addresses.

Class of Networks, such as A, B, and C are now subnetted as classless numbers. Meaning that we are no longer bound by such a strict addressing scheme. Meaning an address that appears to be a Class A address can now be subnetted with 24 bits as opposed to 8. As this was the former rule. Well that's enough of numbers for now. We will review more later on the LABS Section. Now let's move on to Switching!

Chapter 4

SWITCHING

BASIC SWITCHING

Quite a while back, when I cared, and had more hair, we used devices called *HUBS*. Yes, I know that does tend to date me, but there it is. A hub was a very simple device that allowed you to plug in multiple devices and gave those devices a physical path to send data. It was just like a large splitter. You know, like the ones you went to the big box store to buy so you could get a cable TV connecting in another room of the house.

Hubs were the workhorses of the early small networks. It allowed you to connect all of your PC's together and maybe a printer as well. Remember back at the start of the book I talked about the OSI model. Well, this Hub was a device that was at the first layer, the Physical Layer. It allows a *PHYSICAL PATH* to make the connection between your devices. Great, awesome, but there was a small problem with hubs; they didn't have any kind of memory or processing capabilities. So when a frame came from port 1 on the hub and was headed for port 4, the hub would have to poll each port, and ask, "Hey is this frame for you?" So every time a frame went into one of the ports on the hub, that device really had no idea where to send the frame. It was just a plain splitter.

This did not adversely affect small little groups of devices such as a 4 port hub, but it made things slow when you wanted to have more devices on your LAN. Also, it worked in a way that today's Network Admin would never tolerate. The hub worked in what is called *HALF DUPLEX*. That meant that a conversation between two devices looked like two people on Walkie Talkies. "Hey did you get those 100 Frames that I sent?"

"Why yes, yes I did, can you send more?" Each of the devices waiting for the other to finish "talking" before they get to have a go at it. Contrast that to today's switching devices. The modern switch can send data at the same time as receiving data. This is known as *FULL DUPLEX*.

The other real and very common problem was that devices on the hub connection would attempt to send data at the same time as another device. This is called a collision. It's not a good thing. The devices involved in this mishap would be forced to resend their data.

HISTORY 101

A little side note here for the history buffs. Prior to the advent of a usable commercial switch in the early 1990's, hubs and like devices were thought of as just a bridging mechanism. The big traffic in large Campus Backbones was designed to flow through the "Backplane" of a very, very expensive Cisco Router. Or through an FDDI Network Ring topology. The Router was a layer 3 device and was really thought of as a vastly superior way to move data around a large campus. Hubs were known to cause traffic flow problems because of the polling or broadcast nature of the device. So in 1990 the first switch was born. It was manufactured by a company called Kalpana. They introduced a seven port switch into the market. It cost over $10,000. Due to vast improvements to the way data was now moving, these devices, while expensive, were very popular. Oh, by the way, Kalpana was bought by Cisco Systems in 1994. Ka-Ching! I love history.

TODAY'S LAYER 2 SWITCH

I call it a layer 2 switch, because if you're a networking beginner, you may be surprised to know that switches can reside at other layers. There are layer 3 switches, and there are even layer 7 switches. I would like to reserve the deep exploration of those devices to future texts.

Let's talk about what makes the switch an important part of our network, and how works this mystery box. Some advanced switches have a huge array of features, while others may have fewer. For right now we will cover the basics.

The first thing I can say about this device is that when I was introduced to it myself, it was called an intelligent hub. The intelligent part of this equation is simple and elegant. The switch has the ability to actually learn what device is plugged into a specific port. So when an Ethernet cable is run from the network adapter on a PC into a port on a Layer 2 switch, and starts to move data, the switch will copy the MAC Address of the PC into its own internal table. This table is called a MAC Table. Most of the time, switches look at the source MAC address. This is called *SOURCE PORT LEARNING*. It was in this fashion that the device would eventually learn which MAC address was associated with a particular port on the switch. In this way a PC on port one wanted to send something to a device on another port, that device would no longer have to be polled, as in "Hey is this your data?" The data is just forwarded because the switch now knows the MAC address of the receiver.

Another quick note. In the world of Layer 2, the data is in a format known as a frame. Two fields in that Frame are Source

MAC address, and Destination MAC address. The switch is reading these fields.

So we can see that this is a vast improvement in the way data is moved from one port to another. The switch has a frame destined for port 4, and then it just gets delivered to that port and that port alone. Other ports are not involved in this transaction, and when data is returned to the sender from port 4, the same process happens again. The destination MAC address is gleaned from the frame and off it goes.

Alright let's look at another improvement over the hub.

Today's switches operate at very high speeds. In the 90's the maximum speeds for data movement was around 10 Mbps. That's Mega Bits per Second. In the late 90's we moved up to 100 Mbps. Now most switches can operate at Gigabit speed. Clearly that's a good thing. Today's users are using large files and downloading entire movies at the same time while playing their X-Box live and complaining about lag times as they shoot at their buddies in some game. Bunch of Whiners. Hey, try doing that on a Packard Bell with a 14.4 modem!

NEW TERM: BROADCAST DOMAIN

This is the area, or boundary of a broadcast.

A switch will learn the MAC addresses of devices connected to it. But it can never learn the destination of a broadcast. In Layer 2 the broadcast destination looks like this. FF:FF:FF:FF:FF:FF. This is written in Hex. All F's when converted into binary looks like this. 11111111.11111111.11111111.11111111.11111111.11111111.

Wow, if you saw it in decimal it would be, 255.255.255.255.255.255. It's a 48 bit long address. The switch will not put it in the MAC table. So instead, it will send a broadcast to all other ports. It will not go back into the port which it originated. So, in essence, a switch forwards or "floods" broadcasts. The same broadcast will not pass a router. A router does not forward broadcasts.

NEW TERM: COLLISION DOMAIN

This is the area where collisions can occur. Think of the best ride at the carnival *EVER*: the bumper cars ride. It's one big collision domain. All of the cars can run into every other car. So if you have twenty bumper cars do you have a possibility of 20 collisions? Nope. Each car can hit 19 other cars. So that would give us 380 possible collisions. If we installed an early bridge that gave us two collision domains, what would happen? We have 10 cars that can hit 9 other cars for each domain. Now we are down to 90 collisions. Two domains give us 180 possible crackups. So now we can see that the more collision domains we have, the better off we are. During the days of the hub there were collisions on the network constantly. Modern Switches due not suffer from collisions, as each connected device has an access method; CSMA/CD that pretty much eliminates collisions. Each switch port is its own collision domain. Only one car in the bumper car ride. Nothing to run into. In brief, CSMA/CD is an Access Method used by wired computers. They sort of listen to the cable to see if there is currently any data being moved on that particular segment. If it thinks that the cable is clear of traffic then the device will send out the data frame, along with a "JAM" signal to tell other devices that the "Medium", the cable, is busy with traffic.

NEW TERM: STP SPANNING TREE PROTOCOL

This protocol (rule) is designed for switches. You may recall I mentioned that switches will never learn the destination address of a broadcast. That is by design. The switch will forward that broadcast to every port other than the incoming port. This is normal. But, as I also mentioned, broadcasts can slow down a network and cause delays. Many network administrators like to have redundancy built into the design. What I mean by that is they may place an additional switch into the design to allow a separate path to a particular network segment. It's a good idea to have redundancy. The problem arises when there is more than one way to get data somewhere. A broadcast would have more than one way to go, so it would go both ways. And in actuality, it would keep going, round and round. We should try to remember that while Broadcasts are needed for a local device to find another local device, they are forwarded by the Switch. Again, a switch will forward, or flood a broadcast. See the Super Basic drawing one below.

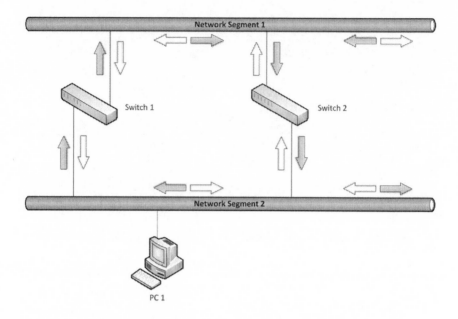

In the above drawing, we see a broadcast being sent by PC1 that resides on Segment 2. We see that the designer of the network has given us more than one path to both segments. Therefore, the broadcast will go to both switches, and the switch will forward that broadcast. The problem is that the broadcast will travel on the path of the gray arrows as well as the path of the white arrows. The end result will lead to what is commonly called a *BROADCAST STORM*. The switch will just keep receiving the broadcast and keep forwarding it. Let's say that on SW1 the original frame is received on Port 1. It then sends out the frame on Port 4. The gray arrows represent that direction. But we also sent the frame to Port 1 on SW2; that's on the red side. We can follow the white arrows all the way back to SW1, and port 4, and because the switch cannot learn the destination port of a broadcast frame, it will send it to port 1. The default behavior is to just keep forwarding the frame. That's not a good thing.

The solution for this problem is the protocol STP. I think it would be easier to go over what it does, rather than how it does it. The switch will actually go through a few steps before a port is allowed to move data. Initially a port will be placed into a *BLOCKING STATE*. It will not forward frames. After this state, the switch will listen to other switches through the STP protocol. This will let the switch understand who is connected to which segment. That state is called learning. If there is no redundant path through that particular port, then the port will move into the forwarding state. It all happens very, very fast.

On the EdgeRouter, on the status tab, you can see the column that says STP state. It will show what that individual port is doing. Whether it is blocking, or learning, or forwarding. In short, STP will stop loops from forming, and that in turn stops the dreaded broadcast storm. And another thing, you can turn this feature off for the device. If in fact you do not have a redundant path for data, then the STP protocol is not needed. There is another version of STP, called RSTP. It is not too important at this time to go over all the granular stuff. It is a more advanced version of the STP protocol.

HARDWARE SWITCHING

You may occasionally hear the term Hardware Switching. This term refers to the piece of hardware that does much of the heavy lifting for a switch. It is known as an ASIC. It is a hardware chip built into each and every physical port on a switch. It's kind of like having a separate CPU for each port. The ASIC does the job of MAC address learning, and the placing of that MAC address into the MAC Table. This allows the movement of data to be very fast.

Most switches operate at what is termed *WIRE SPEED*. That means that they really don't slow down data as it is being passed along the network. ASIC is an abbreviation for *APPLICATION SPECIFIC INTEGRATED CIRCUIT*. A few select Ubiquiti routers will have a *SWITCH CHIP*. They are: ERPoE-5, ER-X, ER-X-SFP and the EP-R6. Using the switch feature on these devices will not affect the CPU. This is a great feature for the home and small office users. I use a EdgeRouter X as my home router.

A new personal side rant: There are many devices that allow both routing and switching features on the same device. That may work fine for SOHO implementations, but I prefer a physical switch, rather than a small router, or modem, to sort things out. Those devices can act like a switch, but lack an ASIC, so any of the heavy lifting is going to happen on the CPU of the device. That does indeed take a toll on the performance of the device.

The same concept holds true for me in other areas as well. A small, home based router handles other duties, like firewalling, very well.

This does not scale to a larger network. If my LAN is 1000 users, I probably want to include a hardware based switching and firewall solution. A hardware firewall is dedicated to that specific task. This makes it highly effective. Ubiquiti has a great firewall. The Unifi Security Gateway is built for that task alone. Ubiquiti currently has two models, and they will handle both SOHO Networks and larger ones as well.

Once again, I am not a salesman for Ubiquiti. I don't make any profit on any equipment, but I've been around long enough to know good from average.

A BIT OF INTERNAL GRANULARITY

Due to the vast differences between various models of switches, I want you to have a few more topics under your belt before we move ahead to configuration. For this text, we will be walking through the configuration of the Toughswitch models. These are the Toughswitch POE and the Toughswitch Pro. The larger and more powerful Edge switches will be covered in volume two.

Remember we are still talking about Layer two devices. At this layer we can also detect errors. A switch can aid in this process by actually looking at the individual frame it is handling. It can check to see if the frame is the correct size. There are internal switching mechanisms in place on some devices that are very complex. This may be too much to ask for the beginning student to completely understand. The frame at Layer two has mechanisms built in so errors can be detected. For now, I just want you to know that a switch can look at the traffic going through a port and be able to tell if a packet is valid, and does not contain errors. It is also the fastest part of your LAN. Offering high port speeds and mostly error free use. Those folks over at Kalpani saw the need and drove the rest of us into the future. Thanks guys.

VLANs

In chapter 1 I talked about the OSI reference model, and how different devices, such as switches and routers, see data in a different way.

VLAN is short for Virtual LAN. A LAN needs a Network ID, and all the devices in that LAN generally can communicate with every other device on the LAN. If you think about all these devices that need to communicate on our network, they share the network address space.

But what if we wanted to have a separate network on that same LAN? One that was physically in the same area but having a subset of those devices only talking amongst themselves. Back in the earlier times we would have been forced to install another router. That would be costly. This device is designed to separate different networks right? And why would we want another network? See, there is a why in there somewhere.

You might want to have a separate network for security purposes. Maybe you have a Human Resource Department that contains sensitive data that you want to segregate from the rest of the employees. Or maybe you want a security camera network, or a separate network for Voice over IP Phones. Maybe I don't want your chocolate in my peanut butter. There are lots of reasons, and you can think of these additional networks as separate subnets. Then again, all these smaller networks reside in larger networks, and still need to have a network ID that is for that sub-network alone. More importantly, these devices will broadcast to the devices on their own network. I want to simplify even further.

BROADCASTS ARE NOT ALWAYS A GOOD THING

When a device on a given network sends out a broadcast, it may be asking for a new IP address, or maybe it is sending out an ARP request, or it might be a print device advertising its own availability. Whatever type it is, it tends to clog the arteries of the LAN. Other devices will hear these broadcasts, and attempt to discern whether that particular call over the network is directed at them. This slows things down a little bit. Just a little really, but when you multiply that over hundreds of devices, the network can get a little chatty. On a LAN of 867 devices, one device may be sending out a broadcast. Well 866 other devices will "hear" that information, and they will have to decide if that information is supposed to be for them. That is a large group of devices just processing data that is not even addressed to them. It would be the same thing as being in a crowded classroom, and having somebody walk in and make an announcement about the bus schedule. Some of the people in the class do not need that information, as they don't use the bus. But they had to process it anyway. And all of that took some time off the CPU clock.

In essence, you cannot have huge groups of devices sharing the same Network ID. They will also share the ability to hear all the broadcast traffic. Broadcasting, while needed for some services, does not scale. By using VLANs that are on the router, and the switch will be able to forward data for the correct VLAN to the associated port.

VLANS create separate broadcast domains. A broadcast from VLAN ID 10, will not *HEAR* a Broadcast from VLAN 20, even if these two VLANS are physically connected to the same switch. That is a real good thing.

A VLAN is identified by a VLAN ID. It's just that, it identifies the VLAN. It's a number, but there is usually a name you can assign as well. It's just a name for the VLAN that will aid in understanding which is which, for example; VLAN 10 is named *SECURITY CAMERAS*.

VLAN ID number 1 is usually reserved for what is known as the *MANAGEMENT VLAN*. By default on most switches, every port is assigned to the VLAN ID number 1. This is called the management VLAN. Think about that a bit. By default, without changing anything. Heck just plug the switch in and go, and all the ports can *SEE* each other. They are in the same VLAN. On an EdgeRouter you can have thousands of VLANS. You probably will not need that many though. We use the *MANAGEMENT VLAN*, to do just that; be able to access devices out there on the network and manage them, manage the crap out of them! You can check for failures and errors, and that sort of fun stuff.

Let's move on to the actual configuration. I also want to point out the various bells and whistles along the way.

THE TOUGHSWITCH PRO

This device from Ubiquiti is aptly named, it is very tough. Designed to be placed at dirty, dusty, hot and cramped wiring closets near you. Stuck in tiny H-boxes at the bottom of towers; that kind of place. It runs, and runs and runs. This is not a device that you have to fret over. I am willing to bet that most readers have restarted networking equipment in their own home at least twice in the last few months. You will not have to do this with this device. Nope.

FIRST TIME ACCESS

The ToughSwitch is a PoE (Power over Ethernet) managed switch. It's designed to push power out through the port interfaces. The basic ToughSwitch PoE can push 24 volts of power out any or all of the connected ports. It has five gigabit ethernet ports and one management port that does not have PoE. This extra management port can be very helpful, in that you can connect a computer up to it for testing connectivity to other devices on the switch.

The ToughSwitch Pro has eight ports, plus a management port, and it can push 24 volt Passive PoE, or 48 volts of standard PoE out any of the eight connected ports.

PoE is short for Power over Ethernet. It is a clever and effective way to power devices that are connecting through the switch. Passive POE just means that the ToughSwitch does not check to see if the connected device is able to handle that power. So when connecting access points or radios, or whatever device you are using, just make sure that the device will handle the power you are going to send it. There are IEEE standards for PoE. One is noted as 802.3af, the other is 802.3at. The first standard, 802.3af was released in 1999 and gave us up to 15.4 watts of power per port. It's a 48 volt standard and it was released back when our network infrastructure was primarily based on Cat3 cable. 15.4 watts was pretty much maxing out the Cat3 cable.

In 2005 the 802.3at standard was released, (actually it's an amendment, but most people refer to it as a standard, so we'll just go with that). With 802.3at the amount of power now available on any port is 30 watts. That's why sometimes 802.3at is referred to as PoE+. It can deliver twice as much power per port as switches that are 802.3af compliant. Another cool thing about 802.3at is that it can categorized devices that need less power and only send what is needed to lower power intensity devices, thus lowering the overall power consumption of the switch.

You really have to pay attention when you are using 24 volt passive PoE with Ubiquiti switches and devices. Passive PoE means it passively, or a better term may be, without intervention, send power down the line, so whether your device needs power or it doesn't, it's going to get it. You need to check your devices to ensure that you are using the proper voltage required. If your AP, or camera require 48 volt PoE it won't hurt it to receive 24 volts, it just won't power it up. On the other hand, if your switch has a port configured for 24 volts and you plug your computer into that port, you are going to start smelling this strange smell of silicone burning. It doesn't matter how fast you pull that ethernet cable out of your computer; that power is travelling at near speed of light, and anyways, once you smell it, it's too late, you have fried your ethernet card. Fortunately, in most cases, you will only need a new network interface card and not a whole new computer. So, just go ahead and get on Amazon and order up a USB ethernet card. They're about $40.00. Oh, and you can get one that won't allow power on it, so you probably want to get that one, seeing how you are now becoming an expert at switching.

Before you connect to the switch, I want to point out that on the front of the switch you will see a port on the far left side labeled *MANAGEMENT*. That port can indeed connect and pass traffic to the other ports, but will do so at limited speeds of 10/100. This port is designed for what is called *OUT OF BAND MANAGEMENT*. What that means is that the switch will not allow any user connected to the other ports to access the management program for the switch. We will see where to set this up in a little bit.

You also will see a USB port built into the switch. According to Ubiquiti that port is reserved for future use. It does have power, so feel free to charge your phone on it.

Also on the front of the switch just above the port there are two little LED's that will light up. There is one on the left and one on the right. What do they indicate? The light on the left side is the indicator for PoE. If it shows a green light that means the device is pushing power. Green is good!

The light on the right is an indicator of link and speed. If the light is amber, it means that the switch sees something connected at the other end of the cable, and is connecting at the speed of 10/100. If the amber light is blinking, that indicates that the port is moving data at those speeds. If the light is Green (Green Is *GOOD*), then you are connected at 1000 Mbps. And again, if it is flashing green, that shows the port is moving data at that speed.

Let's review:

- GREEN IS GOOD!

- KEEP LOCAL TRAFFIC OFF THE MANAGEMENT PORT.

Moving on.

The ToughSwitch has an IP address of 192.168.1.20. Let's connect up and check it out. Go ahead and plug an Ethernet cable into any of the ports of switch and... *WAIT!* Don't plug it into a port if the PoE indicator is amber. Ok, just making sure. Now enter the address into your browser.

As a reminder, if you do not have a router connected on this network, which you will not have if you're only connected to the switch, you are going to need to have a static IP address put in for your ethernet connection.

Remember how to do that? Go to your IPv4 settings on your ethernet connection and change it from *OBTAIN AN IP ADDRESS AUTOMATICALLY* to *USE THE FOLLOWING IP ADDRESS*. Then use an IP address of 192.168.1.x where x is equal to anything up to 254, except 20 since that is the IP address of the switch and using the same number will cause a conflict.

NAVIGATION OF THE SWITCH

When you put the IP address of the switch into the browser address bar and press enter, you will get a login screen. The default username and password combo is ubnt/ubnt. Once you log in you will then see the management interface.

From left to right you will see the tabs labeled: STATUS, DEVICE, PORTS, VLANS and ALERTS.

Let's check these out, one at a time.

Just a note before you get lost in all the granular stuff. If you just want to connect stuff together such as a PC and a printer, there is no need to go into the management screen. Just plug in your stuff and go. This device will pass traffic from port to port without having to set anything.

STATUS TAB

This is the main tab, and its purpose is to give you an overall view of Link-Status, Network settings, current settings, and statistics.

Under the Status section you will see the device name, its location, the date, the current uptime (since last boot), and the Mac address of the switch.

The next section will show Port status, which is pretty self-explanatory. It shows whether an interface is up and running, and if you are sending voltage down that port (PoE) and STP status and MTU. There is also Port Statistics area just underneath. It is in this area you can view traffic being moved by the switch. You can get a pretty granular view of errors here as well. You will also see the option of Raw/Formatted to view the actual data. The Raw format will have more detail. There is the RX side for receive information, and a TX side for sending data. You can see total packets sent or received, and you can see total errors sent or received.

In general, errors listed here are important to note. If you see a small number of errors, and that number stays pretty stable, then breathe easy. If these errors dramatically increase in number then you may have a problem. These errors may be caused by connected devices, or the cable itself may be damaged. I have seen Cat5 cable runs where there was an actual knot in the cable run. And while the budget cable tester may have shown that there is connectivity, it cannot show probable errors.

Recall that STP is used to prevent Broadcast loops from forming. And you can see on this Status tab whether or not the particular port is using STP. My advice is to turn it off if you have a flat network, and there is not a redundant path for data to flow. What I mean by flat is a topology that does not have a redundant path.

Ok, the next area in this tab is the Total Throughput information area. Total throughput will show information both as a graph, and as a number. Next to this we see Data Distribution. This is represented as a Pie chart. (I love pie.) By the way, this pie chart will update itself. If you want to see even more detail, click on the graphical image of the port itself (it will turn blue). And you should then be able to view Packet Rate, Packet Distribution, and Throughput for that individual port. To return to the default view select the, Show Device Details.

DEVICE TAB

This Tab allows us to set many parameters that are very important, so I want to move through them one at a time.

FIRMWARE UPDATE

Here you will see the current Firmware version of your switch. The version name will start with SW. You should always try to keep the firmware of your devices current. You will see the build number here as well.

The firmware itself refers to software, or code, that is placed onto an actual chip. The build numbers refer to the version of that software. For us, we should concern ourselves with having the most recent firmware.

You can also set whether you want to have the device search for updates, or you can download and supply the firmware updates manually. To manually check for updates just click the check now button. Now, the update process is a three-step thing. First you select Choose File, to find the file that you downloaded. Then you click Open on the file. Then you want to select Upload. Then Click Update to confirm all this. Then go get some coffee to go with that pie, because this will take a few minutes. DO NOT TURN ANYTHING OFF! By the by, if you made a large amount of changes to the Switch, do not worry as they will still be there after a Firmware Upgrade. Yay!

MANAGEMENT NETWORK SETTINGS

In this section you can either statically assign the switch an IP address, or you can allow a DHCP server to assign the device an address, or you can leave it just like it is. You see, this is a Layer 2 device. It cares not about the IP address. You give this switch an address merely to manage it, to log into it and set up cool stuff. You can give this job to a DHCP server, but I recommend giving this some thought. I usually assign addresses that I have laid out ahead of time, to devices that I want to open up and fiddle about. Just as long as it's in your regular range of IP addresses. If you leave it alone, it will have the default address of 192.168.1.20. I recommend that you change it. Too many other devices may have the same default IP address, so we don't want any confusion out there. In fact many Ubiquiti products will have that same address. So if you never change it, there may be an address conflict that you don't want, and another thing, if you use DHCP to allocate the address to the device you will not know that address. You would have to use the Discovery tool to know what address is assigned so I do not advise you to rely on DHCP.

You will also see the checkbox labeled Management Port only here. If you select that box you will only be able to manage the device while connected to the port on the front labeled Mgmt. Using this port will provide you with a little more security, as nosy users will be unable to open up a GUI session with your Switch. If you want to use the Mgmt port to actually move traffic you must not check this box. Also be aware that the port will only move traffic at 10/100 speeds, and can actually impair the performance of the switch.

On the right-hand side, you will see the entry for the Gateway IP. This is the port that is upstream of the switch. Usually a Router or a DSL Modem that will connect you to the internet. The default address is 192.168.1.1. Under this you will see the entry for the DNS address. As I mentioned before, DNS is the Web Name to IP address resolver that we need to go online. You will see a Primary entry and a Secondary entry. If, for some reason, the Primary DNS server is unable to answer your query, a secondary will then be used in place of the Primary. I use the public DNS of Google at 8.8.8.8.

BASIC SETTINGS

In this area you will set the name of the switch, the Time Zone and the location. You can optionally set the Latitude and Longitude.

As I have ranted on previously, you should set the name of the switch to something that makes sense to you. This device name will show up in the Discovery tool as well as any Network Management Software that you might be using. You can also enter a location, like Main Office. You will also be setting the Time Zone here. The default setting is Western Europe, so if you live in Pittsburg, change it. The final option here is the Lat and Long. There are several free online tools to help you find these numbers such as www.latlong.net. Have fun.

MANAGEMENT CONNECTION SETTINGS

These are the settings used for connection to the switch. The first section is WEB SERVER. Here you can select how you are connecting. If you want to use a secure connection you will just check the box. The port is also listed here so if you want to change it you may do so. Just don't forget what you changed it to. If you are not using a secure connection then it is just http: and that uses port 80. The last little bit is the Session timeout. The default is 15 minutes. If your session expires you have to login again.

The next section is SSH. This is to be able to log into the device using a program like Putty. Under here you can see and change the port being used, you can also import an SSH Key File. The option Password Authentication is selected by default. If you deselect it you will have to use a SSH Key File. If you don't use a Key file, then you will be prompted for the Administrative credentials when logging in. Aspects of the SSH Key is beyond the scope of this text. It will be covered in Volume 2.

The final Option here is using TELNET. The default setting is off. Telnet is not recommended. It does not have the ability to have a secure connection, and all traffic passes in clear text, so someone running a packet sniffing program could easily discover your username and password combo.

SERVICES: This area is for setting up SNMP agent, System Log, Dynamic DNS and NTP client.

SNMP: I have mentioned this Protocol before, but let's zip through it. This basically allows your switch to send alerts to another device that may analyze these agents, and let the admin know something may be broken or otherwise is an unwanted state. We have the SNMP Agent, which basically tells the device to collect data to send off, and we have the Community String which functions as a sort of Password to authenticate to the SNMP server. The default is "public". We have Contact, as in who should be notified that the device is having a problem, and we have Location. In larger Networks the administrators rely on NMS, or Network Management Software to collect and sort data. These devices poll, or talk to network devices, and record that information. There are lots of NMS products out there.

DYNAMIC DNS: This is a service that allows mapping of a name to an IP address that may change. Let's say I have a Mail Server at my house. I want users of my mail server to resolve or FIND the server at the name www.kevinsmailserver.com. There is no such server, but I digress. If my service provider was to change the address on the WAN side of my router, then you would no longer find my mail server. Dynamic DNS is a service that keeps track of the changing IP address, and will update the Name to Address association. There are lots of Dynamic DNS services out there on the WEB. Some are free. If you were using this service in your network you will have to enter the name of the service, the username and password.

SYSTEM LOG: In this area you will enable or disable the System log. By default it is disabled. If you enable it, all of the log messages will be seen on the Alerts Tab. You also have the ability here to send these alerts off to another device. You need the IP address of the device you are sending them to, and you need to configure the device to accept those messages.

Each log entry will contain information that shows the time of the event, the host it came from, and a level of the alert: informational, error, and warning. Stuff like that. Hidden in the background are services that generate these alerts. Different services will have different levels of detail about the event. I would say "Problem," but really it's more accurate to say event. Kind of like, "I've fallen, and I can't get up." "Port One is Down."

These logs can get rather verbose. So be aware.   •

NTP: NTP stands for Network Time Protocol. It is used to synchronize the clocks of devices on a network. If you enable the system log, then the time is used to let you know when something happened. You can select whether you want the device to get the time from a Time Server. On the next line you can select the actual server that you want to use. The default is 0.ubnt.pool.ntp.org. It's a good idea to set this up.

SPANNING TREE: We talked about this little nugget awhile back. Remember that this STP protocol is going to give us redundancy of our network while avoiding any Broadcast Loops. The settings are pretty basic. You can enable or disable. If you enable it then you have the choice to select from STP or RSTP. RSTP is Rapid STP. Guess what? It's faster, use it.

On the right we have the settings, MAX AGE, which is how long the switch will keep the configuration it knows about. If it does not hear any new config messages coming in, it will attempt to reconfigure itself.

HELLO TIME is how often a device will let everyone know its personal configuration.

FORWARD DELAY is the time that a device will wait before it starts forwarding data out a port after it has "Learned" the Topology.

The PRIORITY VALUE is something that is used when the devices on the LAN need to figure out the best way to send some data. This will help elect the Root Bridge. Fancy talk for the switch that is being used, and the port on the switch that is used to forward data, if there is more than one path to possibly take. Refer to SuperBasic Drawing one.

JUMBO FRAMES: This setting is used if you are using Gigabit Ethernet connections. If you are on Gigabit, then select this option.

DEVICE DISCOVERY: This will allow the device to be seen with the Discovery tool.

SYSTEM ACCOUNTS: Here is the spot to change the Administrator's Name and Password. To change the password, you will need the old one. Password length should be 8 characters.

DEVICE MAINTENANCE: Here you can reboot the device. Remember any changes not saved will not be there when you reboot. Support info is a way to generate a file that Ubiquiti would request when they need to look into some problems. Moving on.

CONFIGURATION MANAGEMENT: Ok, this stuff is important. This is the place you want to go to back up your device. You do this by selecting Back Up Configuration. You will want to store that file in a secure location as it will have sensitive stuff like passwords and so on.

The Upload Configuration is for installing new configs on your switch. These files don't like to go from other switches, so only use files from the same kind of switch. Do not attempt to upload a ToughSwitch 5 PoE to a ToughSwitch 8 PoE. Get your chocolate out of my Peanut Butter!

RESET TO FACTORY DEFAULTS: You should always make a backup copy before doing this. This indeed sets the switch back to all defaults.

Hey that's the end of that Big Tab-O-fun. Let's move to the next.

THE PORTS TAB

In this Tab you will access the individual functions of the ports.

The first thing you see is an overview of all the ports. The image will display the active ports, and connections. For each port you can see the Status, PoE, Link Speed, PING Watchdog, STP, and Alerts.

Placing your mouse over these ports will show you these settings

To change a Port's settings just click on it. You can save these changes, revert changes, and you can also test changes. If you don't click the Apply button after 180 seconds everything goes back to the way it was. You can also Clone setting to all the other ports. OK, just a reminder that if you make PoE changes, they get cloned as well, so make sure that connected devices support the PoE that you are sending out of that port.

BASIC SETTINGS: Here you can enter a name for the port. You can also enable or disable it. If you disable it, the PoE setting will remain. You can enable PoE. The ToughSwitch 8 uses both 24v and 48v. The ToughSwitch 5 PoE only has settings for 24v.

You can select link speed here. The default setting is Auto. And the switch is smart enough to detect the correct speed, so this is a safe setting. You can also change the settings for Flow Control, but it's on for a good reason. It allows the port to manage data rates. It's a good idea to leave it on.

PING WATCHDOG: This utility is only for PoE enabled ports. Basically it will ping a device on a known IP address. If for some reason the device does not answer the Pings, then the switch can cut the power to that device, forcing it to reboot. "TRY TURNING OFF YOUR ROUTER AND TURNING IT ON AGAIN." That sentence is the entire first day of training at your local Service Provider.

The ping interval is how often you are pinging a device. The delay is how long it waits before starting all this up, and the failure count is how many times the ping has to fail before the switch cuts the power. Use a ping interval that takes into consideration that the device may be in the process of rebooting after an update.

Remember, losing power during an update may brick your device.

SPANNING TREE SETTINGS FOR PORT

Here you can select Edge Port, Priority and Path Cost. Edge Port should be selected when you know that the port only connects to a host, and that Host in turn is not connected to another switch or router. It should not be selected if the port is connected to another switch or router.

The value Path Cost is something that you can set manually. Let's say that this is a Gigabit connection. If you set the Path Cost to 0 (the lower the better), then that path will be used. If all Path Costs are the same then the tie breaker is Priority. Again, the lower number wins this contest. STP will consider Path Cost when trying to calculate the best path. So again, if there are equal path costs then the Priority value is used to determine the best path. Priority can be set from 0 to 255.

CONFIGURE ALERTS FOR PORT

Here you can set predetermined values. Bandwidth above or below a certain count; link going down, etc. These are pretty basic. I would not get too enamored of the Bandwidth settings. Remember, the log file can get pretty large pretty fast, and it makes for some boring reading.

THE VLAN TAB

I'm sure all of you have read and re-read the section above on VLANS. Well here is the place on the switch where we get to set them up. For our purposes, I am going to try to keep it simple. There are many exceptions to the settings that I want you to consider, so bear with me. I will discuss the most *COMMON* setup of this Tab.

Here you will click the Add button to add your VLAN. This would have been created on your router. So let's say that you have a VLAN 100. It's going to be used for some security cameras. You will click Add, and then enable it. Then you will fill in the VLAN ID. This is the number 100. You can then add the name *CAMERA VLAN*, under the Comment section. You do not want to make this VLAN the Management VLAN. Doing so will disconnect you from the switch. You would then have to reset it to defaults to get access again. From here you can specify what port is going to be moving your VLAN traffic. You can select Tag, Untag, or

Exclude. Exclude tells the port that you are excluding a VLAN from accessing that port. So that would not be the correct setting for our Camera VLAN. Tag keeps the VLAN tag information in the frame, and Untag removes that Tag. If the port is being sent to a PC for example, then it should be Untagged. The Management Port will be excluded. If the device is something smart like a VOIP phone, something that understands VLANS, then the selection is Tagged.

In the case of the Camera VLAN, we want it to be selected as Untagged. Untagged generally means that the device is part of that VLAN, and Tagged is another way to send data to another switch or network segment. Like I said, it is not always that way. IP Phones are one exception. They have the ability to see tagged packets. Just make sure to check to see if your particular device is VLAN aware.

A trunk port is one that is passing all VLAN data, so if you had 3 VLANS on your router, and the router is connected to the switch on Port 2, then you will Trunk all VLANS on that port.

You may need to do a little research to find out if your devices should belong to an Untagged, or a Tagged port. In general, PC's and other similar devices will be on an Untagged Port. The switch removes the VLAN ID information from the packet before handing it to the

PC. You also have the choice here to delete a VLAN. On 115

the larger Edge Switches there is a VLAN wizard. It will show all of the VLANS, and all the Untagging, tagging stuff on the main screen. It will also show the *TRUNK* ports. Trunk ports are the selected ports that will carry all of the VLAN info downstream to the next device if needed. If I have several switches that each has devices on different VLANS, then the port that interconnects the two devices would be a *TRUNK* port. It *TAGS* all of the VLANS.

ALERTS TAB

The Alerts Tabs displays alerts or system events. When alerts logging is enabled on the Ports Tab, then the Alert Log will list all the Alerts. Remember by default it's disabled. When you have this set up you will see the options of Select all, and Clear Selected. You can refresh the page or do a search for something specific. Entries that are displayed in the log will include port number and time of the event.

SYSTEM LOG: This one is pretty basic. You get the option of clear and refresh. System logs are pretty vanilla with stuff like, system started, system stopped, system rebooted, along with the date and time.

TOOLS

On the Top right-hand corner of the page you will find the Tools menu. It will give you more insight into the switch. Here you can find out the Mac addresses of attached devices. You can perform a PING test to see if a device responds. You can also perform a TraceRoute Test to trace the hops, or the path taken to a specific device.

Also included here is the Discovery tool. It's very useful.

Well that about covers all the fun little buttons and Tabs in our switch.

As I mentioned earlier, there are several other Ubiquiti switch types. There is the Unifi Switch that is designed to work in the world of Wireless Access Points. There are Edge switches that range from 8 to 48 ports. These switches are loaded with more options than a new car. You literally will see hundreds of choices. From Authentication to security. These advanced devices will be profiled in future volumes.

Chapter 5

FIREWALL AND NAT

Before we get started on configuring our firewall, I want to let you know that we will not be covering every possible setup in the firewall. The simple reason is that there are just too many variables to try to explain. There are many options you can setup in the firewall, and while they are important to understand from a beginner's standpoint, they are not going to be used in every situation. We are going to set up the router with a basic firewall that will protect both our LAN users and the router itself. Moving forward, most beginners will slowly add or refine rules and settings that further define their own network.

FIREWALL NAT TAB

When you open this main tab, you will see four additional tabs. They are PORT FORWARDING, FIREWALL RULES, NAT, and FIREWALL NAT GROUPS.

The first of these is the Port Forwarding tab. What does this do? Well, the purpose of this tab is to allow a device or Host on the external network, (WAN) to access a device on the internal network (LAN), by using the public IP address of the router. This is very useful for certain tasks such as accessing a camera server on the local network from your home network. This way you can check on your security cameras, or just about any kind of service running on a LAN computer.

The settings here are pretty straightforward. There are a few settings that you should know about.

HAIRPIN NAT which is enabled by default, allows a user on the local network to access a device on that same network by using the public IP address of the router. It's a good thing, so leave that selected. It's a good tool to use when testing. Let's take the example of a camera system again. You are on site and you want to test to see if you had configured the remote access to the Network Video Recorder (NVR) correctly. Without Hairpin NAT configured, you would have to go off site to see if you had set up port forwarding correctly. With Hairpin NAT enabled, and assuming that your camera system can be viewed through a web browser, you can simply open a browser and type in the public IP address and the port being used, and you will see if the camera system is available remotely.

AUTO FIREWALL is also enabled by default, and it will create firewall rules and settings for you. If you deselect this box, then you will have to manually create firewall rules for your port forwarding setup to function. You will also select the appropriate LAN and WAN interfaces from the menu. You can add additional LAN interfaces if that is your setup. Let's say that you want to allow access to a server on your network that runs your security camera software. The software allows you to view and move cameras around. Some of these cameras can record images in very low light and some software applications will allow you to point the camera or even adjust the zoom level. The cameras are known as PTZ, for pan, tilt, zoom. Let's say that the internal IP address of the server is 192.168.10.99 and the software is available on port 5127. You are going to make a new rule. Click on new rule. The first entry is the original port. That will be 5127. Next, select the protocol. If you are unsure whether its TCP or UDP, select both. Then you will enter the address of the device you are trying to reach. That is 192.168.10.99, and the associated port which is 5127. You can then give this connection a descriptive name and click apply. That's it.

If you click, SHOW ADVANCED OPTIONS, you will see that the setting Auto Firewall is enabled by default. Remember that this will open the ports on the router to allow this connection. If you look into the FIREWALL POLICIES, you will not see this entry. It will not be shown here, but rest assured that it is indeed working. And remember if you deselect the auto firewall, you will manually have to create a policy that opens the port of 5127 on the router.

The same sort of thing would apply to a Web Server that may reside on your private network. Let's say you have a server holding a web site that is s on your LAN at 192.168.10.199. You would do the exact same steps as before, but enter port 80 as the port, as that's the one that is used for web based traffic. One more thing, if your application uses more than one port you can enter it using a comma or a dash. Like this 5127-5129, or 5127, 5128, 5129. No problem.

Let's dig a little deeper here. There are a few basic things yet to learn. Remember that the router has a connection to the Internet Service Provider (ISP). Let's say that the "Public" address of the Router is 5.1.1.1. and you have the LAN side of the Network as 192.168.10.0/24. The user that wants to access the Camera Server at 192.168.10.99 can only reach the public address of 5.1.1.1. so they would enter the address in their browser as 5.1.1.1:5127. That is the port number after the public address. They would be able to access the software on the server. Hey that sounds pretty simple. Well hold up there Cletus. There are evidently bad people out there on the old interweb. Yup, it's true. They will scan public addresses and ports and attempt to gain access to your LAN by trying to open ports that are normally used by specific software. For example the port 3389 is used for what is known as Remote Desktop. And it is used to allow remote control of a PC, or a server.

If I have the public address of 5.1.1.1 and I have a server on my LAN that I connect to for work, I would do so on port 3389. To stop people from trying to gain access in this way, I change the originating port to another number. For any IP address there are 65536 available ports. Yes, that's the number. You can set up the original port as something like 53989, and then the "forward to" port will be 3389. That will help keep the hackers at bay. Now you know why that selection exists.

FIREWALL POLICIES TAB

We will begin with a few basics. A Firewall Policy is a set of rules with a default action. The rules you create are read and executed from top to bottom in order. When there is a match to one of those rules, we then proceed onto an *ACTION* for that rule. For example, if the rule says, "If cousin Larry knocks at your door, then perform the action of turning off the TV and being very quiet in the hope he wanders off somewhere." So we have a matching condition; cousin Larry knocking on the door, and we have an associated action; turn off the TV.

After all the matches are gone through from top to bottom, we have a default action of *DROP*, *ACCEPT* or *REJECT*. In other words, if there was not a match to a rule, then perform this default action. A rule will basically tell the router what action to take when it processes a particular packet. All of these rules are organized into the *RULE SET*, and these rules are read in order. If a match is made, then an associated action will take place. After all the rules are read and there is no match, that is when the default action will take place. Some of these rules can get very, very specific. I don't want you to get frustrated right off the bat. Firewall rules can be very hard to digest. You will probably lock yourself out of your own device at least once before your realize it. It's ok. That's the best way to learn the process. So, let's start with something simple, like Cousin Larry.

PACKETS

Packets are the little guys that the Router looks at, when it is performing any filtering action. A packet is a portion of the actual data that is moving across the network. If you are connecting to the website of Google.com, then each packet will have information embedded into it such as the destination IP address of Google, and the source address of your network. You are moving a good bit of data when connecting to a Web Site, so there are going to be lots and lots of packets. Each one of these is a very specific size. That way, if a packet shows up at the other end, and it's not the correct size or it's damaged, then it can be resent. Each packet will be much like a page of a very long letter that you are sending. Each of these packets is numbered, and can travel in different directions to reach its final destination. There they are reassembled in the correct numbered order and checked out to make sure they are the right size. A router will do filtering and make routing decisions based on the information in this packet.

PACKET FLOW

Let's all try to remember earlier when I talked about the LAN and the WAN. The LAN was the entire range of local addresses that is used to identify your local devices, and the WAN side consisted of the *PUBLIC ADDRESS* side of the router that connected you to your service provider, and therefore connected you to the largest WAN out there; the internet. So I think it's pretty common to think of traffic flow going from the LAN to the WAN or from the WAN to LAN.

The EdgeRouter looks at flow a little differently. We have three directions for traffic flow. We have IN, we have OUT, and we have LOCAL. The IN direction means that the router is looking at traffic coming in. It could be originating from a local user, or it could be coming from the internet. Rules that apply to the direction IN, are there to protect the router. The traffic coming from the LAN side is traffic coming from a user that is connecting to the router for administration or maintenance. The other type of traffic on the IN is traffic that we originated, or started, the conversation, so we can assume it is safe traffic.

The next direction is OUT, and that means out to the internet provider, and also out to the local users. The LOCAL direction is for traffic coming to the router and then being passed to another physical port of the device to send data to local users. This rule direction is there to protect your LAN while the IN direction is designed to protect the router.

The OUT portion is pretty easy. This is anything going out our ports. Once again, if we trust our LAN users, we don't need to worry too much about the OUT direction. Remember this is traffic originating from the router. The only traffic you would have come back to you from the router is covered by the IN rule, and that is when you are configuring the router. The other part of the OUT traffic is stuff leaving the router and going to the service provider. If the traffic was originated from our trustful users, we don't have to set this up at this point. As I mentioned before, there are boatloads of various reasons that you may indeed someday need to set this up, but for our current discussion we won't need to set this up.

CONNECTION STATES

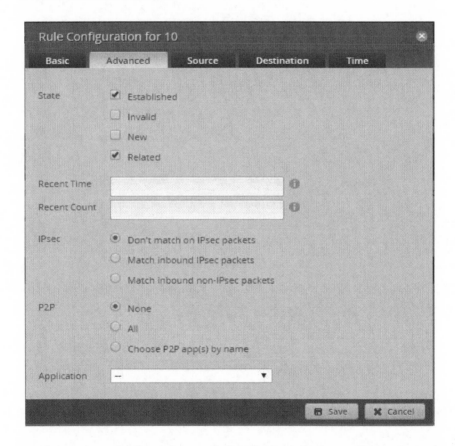

Shown here is the Advanced TAB. We will be walking through this in just a little bit, but for now let's figure out what this does.

You can see here the Category of State, and you have four selections. ESTABLISHED, INVALID, NEW and RELATED.

For our purposes, we will be configuring a basic firewall using these *STATES*. So just what do these settings represent? Traffic that is represented by the State NEW is traffic that is being used to create a new connection. When you open a browser window and open your default web page, that page is receiving a packet from your local PC, and will be labeled *NEW*. New packets should only originate from users, and should not be coming IN to your router. They should also not be coming to your device, so they will not be needed when filtering the LOCAL traffic.

ESTABLISHED and RELATED states go together. This is traffic coming back from that web page to sort of saying, "Hey there, I got your New packet so let's make a connection." ESTABLISHED packets are keeping the connection between the two ends, and you need to accept this traffic. You can select both ESTABLISHED and RELATED states at the same time. Think of it like this. If you connect to the Google home page you have an established connection. All the fun extra stuff on that page like MAPS, NEWS, or GMAIL, is related state traffic.

Ok, so what is INVALID traffic? It's traffic trying to reach you while designated as NEW. Traffic that has your LAN address listed as the source and not the destination. This is traffic that needs to be dropped like a hot rock. A quick side rant.

You have the ability to do several things with packets. If you want to deny them, you have the choice of drop or reject. So what is the difference? Good question. The action of Drop will do just that. It will drop that packet. In comparison, reject will send back a nice little message saying, "Hey I rejected your traffic." It is fair to say that in some cases you may not want the sender to have any idea if the traffic ever arrived. Hence the drop action. Like a hot rock.

Now we are going to do a little step by step, so you will be able to protect your router and your LAN. Let's go. Open the router at its default address of 192.168.1.1. We are going to assume that you have an Internet connection at Eth1 and your local network is 192.168.1.0/24 at that is on ethernet0. I currently have my eth2 configured, so just look at how it is labeled.

My Eth0 is marked Local. When I created the interface, I put that description in to remind me what its connected to. We see that my internet provider is giving me an address of 5.1.1.253. I have it noted as internet. I created a 192.168.2.0 network, and I use that one in my house to test out stuff. The first thing we will do is open the Firewall/Nat Tab and select Firewall Policies.

Create New Firewall Ruleset ✕

Name *	
Description	
Default action *	● Drop
	○ Reject
	○ Accept
Default Log	☐

💾 Save

For our Purposes you will name the first RuleSet WAN_IN. Give it a description. We want to select *DROP* as our default action. If you select the Default Log option you will get a log entry when the default action happens. Now click save. When you do that it will show up in your list, but you can also see that your ruleset is empty. We need to make a couple rules, so on the right hand side select the dropdown Action button. Select edit RuleSet. You will see four tabs. Rules is the default view. You will also see that there are no rules so you are going to add one. Click: Add New Rule.

Once again, feel free to describe your rule. I would call it "Allow established/Related." That's what we are doing first. Select the action of Accept. We need to accept this type of traffic, remember?

Leave All Protocols as All Protocols and leave the logging option off for now. Ok you are done with this tab, so click on the Advanced tab. Click both ESTABLISHED and RELATED as the connection states.

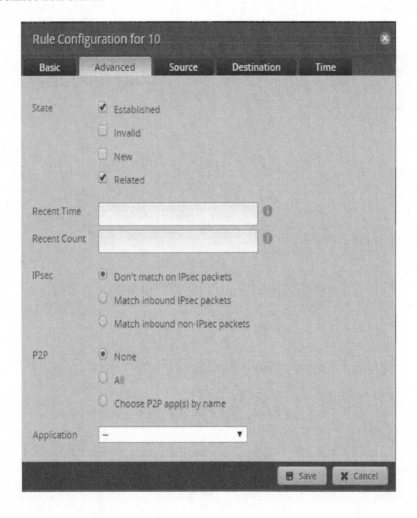

We don't need to use the Source tab, the Destination tab, or the Time tab. Like I said, there are tons of options here. Let's try not to get too crazy. I will have another Firewall Setup in the back of the book, and there will be lots of options used in the volume two tomes.

Click save. Ok, next we can see those tabs next to the rules tab. Click on the Configuration tab. You will see the description that you put in earlier, and you will see the default action that we selected of *DROP*.

Move to the Interfaces Tab. Here you will need to enter the interface that we are firewalling. If you are connected to the internet on Eth1 then you will select Eth1 here. On the right you will select the direction of IN. Well alrighty then. We need another rule. We need the rule to filter our Invalid traffic, so get back to the Rules tab and select Add New Rule. This one we will call *DROP INVALID STATE*. Once it is created then click on the Action button on the right to edit this rule. Click Basic. Once again, we make an entry on the Basic Tab, but this time we enter Drop. On the Advanced Tab we select the connection state of Invalid. We can skip the other tabs here. Now click save. Go back into the Tab marked Interfaces. Select the Interface as Eth1 and the direction of IN. Now click save rule order. Remember that rules are applied one at a time. In this case we have the Invalid rule run second after the Accept rule.

Great, you are halfway there. Now what we need to do is the exact same rules, but we need to apply them to the direction Local, so you will have to add a new Ruleset. Call it WAN_LOCAL. You will need to make the exact same rules but the difference will be on the Direction selection under Ruleset Configuration. All you have to do is make the direction Local. You will repeat the first setup and when you are done you will have two rulesets and each of those will have two rules. It should look like this:

And the Ruleset configuration should look like this. Of course, it may not be the same if you choose a different description, or you select a different Name.

Please note that the Action is Accept on the first and Drop on the second.

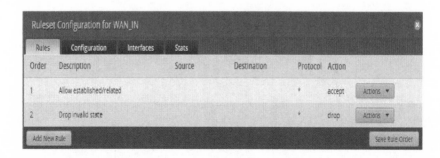

Now a quick lesson for the unsure. It's normal to be wary of incorrectly configured firewalls. Really it is. When you have time, one of the things you might want to do is to run through the WAN to LAN Wizard. When you do, the router will have to be put back to defaults, so back up your current configuration. Anyway, when you setup the router using this wizard, it will load this firewall for you. After it's setup you can go and open the Firewall Tab and look at all the settings. You will find that the default setup is exactly the same steps that you took above.

Let's review a few major things.

A Ruleset is a group of rules. These rules are read one at a time, in order. These rules are basically matching rules. When a match is found then the rule will have an associated action. Once all of the rules are read and there is no match, then the default action will take place. The order of the rules is very critical. This is where some users get into trouble.

Let's pretend you're a doorman at my fancy nightclub. You are my firewall. You are going to filter out the things we may not want entering our club. As such, I give you a list to check for matching conditions. I have some people I don't want in, so they are definitely on the list. Let's say I have the list of people I don't want in, and they are the first rule. No Cousin Larry, nobody in clown makeup, and nobody with the name Cletus. But our list is not really complete yet. I have the matches, and I have the action of deny entry, but I still need an allow list. It could be very simple. I could say, "allow everyone else." That would work. So deny Cousin Larry, anyone named Cletus, and anyone in clown makeup, and then allow everyone else. Rule 1 is the deny, and rule 2 is the allow.

If I wanted to make an exception to this and allow my aunt Ruth in, (I swear she looks like a clown), I cannot make rule 3 allow Aunt Ruth. She would have made a match on the Clown makeup rule in rule 1, and she would have been denied. In this case what we have to do is make the Allow Aunt Ruth in rule 3, and just move it up in the order to run before our No Clown Makeup rule. Order is important. I want to try to explain a real scenario now and no clowns.

Many of you have heard of ICMP. It's a protocol, and one of the utilities that run under it is the PING utility. Many administrators like to block the ICMP protocol coming to the router, aka, the IN direction. They do this to block out what is known as the "PING of Death." Sounds ominous. Basically a "PING of death" is a PING packet that is way bigger than it's supposed to be, so it can jam up your network and do lots of bad things. You should Google "PING of Death."

The admin creates a rule that denies the ICMP protocol. Well, the result of making that his first rule is that users in the LAN who try to ping a website or another device on the outside of the LAN, will not receive an answer because ICMP was blocked. Oops. If he used the Connection States rule, a ping reply would be accepted as it is technically a response from a device that you initiated. It falls under the established/related traffic. You sent a PING, and that packet is labeled NEW. Remember, if it comes from our users we assume it is legit traffic. It is in this case.

And after all this, I want you to understand that firewalls can be very complex, and therefore they can be a little daunting. As we have seen, there are lots of options that we have not even talked about yet. With all those options and variations, you could have hundreds of settings. Some people don't even try to set them up for fear they will make everything worse while others may download one they found on the Interweb. For now, until you gain more experience, stick with the basic firewall that uses Connection States. There will be another sample firewall setup at the back of this book.

NAT TAB

Can you remember back to the basic setup stuff that allowed you to access the internet? Well NAT was one of those key items that you need to setup. NAT stands for Network Address Translation and what it does is allow you to setup a *TRANSLATION*, so you can use the Public IP address to show the internet world as a *SOURCE*, of your traffic. Your private IP address is not usable on the internet, so, in essence, we borrow the Public IP address of the router and that address is shown as being the source of our traffic.

When you crack open the NAT tab, you will see that we have two major sections. At the top we have the box labeled Add Source NAT Rule. A source NAT rule is pretty basic. We are changing our *SOURCE* address from a private IP to that of the Public one. The reason that the NAT tab is located on this Firewall section is that it will act like a firewall. It will have rules and just like a firewall, those rules are going to be read until a match is made. If the match is made, then there will be an action. If there is not a match, we move on to the next rule. Does any of this sound familiar?

Ok, so on the next screenshot we see what happens when you open the selection of Add Source NAT rule. You can see the selections here are rather verbose. Lots and lots of round buttons, square boxes, dropdowns, and menu selections exist here. DO NOT PANIC. Remember, like a new car that my buddy has, it has lots of buttons, but you don't need to use them all to drive the car.

Going back to the stuff we need to set up to get out onto the internet. We are going to change the source address of our packets to become those of the WAN interface. You only need to select a few things to get this to work. You can select a description for this rule. You have the check box to enable or disable this NAT rule. Leave it enabled.

You must choose both the outbound interface and the translation. The outbound interface is the interface of your router that is connected to the WAN; that's outbound. For the translations, you have the choice of Masquerade, or choose the IP address and or Port combination. In most cases you will select Masquerade. It will allow you to use the WAN address, but additionally you will have a unique port assigned to each connection. There are thousands of ports available, so it is my recommended choice here, as is scales very well, meaning you can support lots of connections. The other choice of using a specific address or port is considered Static mapping, or static NAT, and it does not include a mapping of a unique port to each connection. Also, notice that you see a little blue asterisk. That means that this selection is necessary.

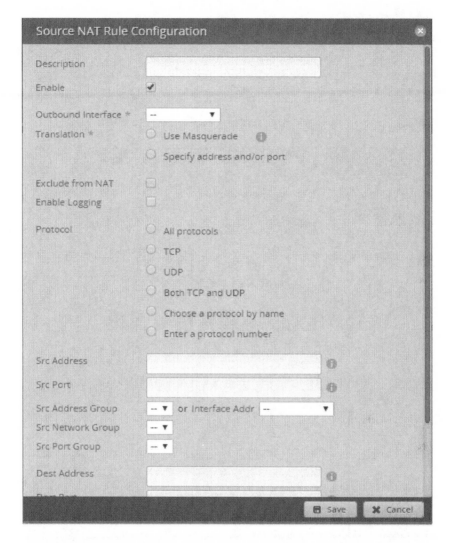

For our purposes, we will stick to using the Translation of Use Masquerade. You have the Exclude from NAT, and enable logging features.

You have the option to select a particular protocol by name or number. You can set the source address or port, as well as the destination address and port.

Included in this huge screen is the option to use or select a port, address, or network group. Ok, like I said, lots of options. Remember what we are doing here. We are selecting the criteria for *MATCHING* our packets, and the *ACTION*, for what we are doing with them. OK, so the matching here for us will be simple.

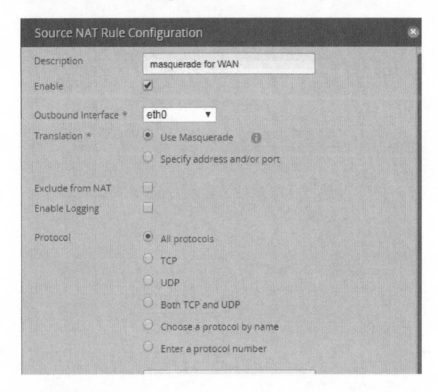

I have left off the bottom of the screen, as I have not selected any of those options. You see I have the Description filled in, I have it Enabled, and I have selected my Outbound Interface of eth0. My translation is Use Masquerade, and I have left the default of All Protocols. What is this doing? Well it is translating everything leaving the router; everything. That is the match, and the action is to translate. Every packet is being given the source address of the public side of the router. Most of the time you will be using this type of setup for your NAT. It is by far the most common.

I would like a sidebar here to talk about the option that you see at the bottom of your screen. The port, network, and the address group items.

DESTINATION NAT

Destination NAT is not used much. Usually when you want to get to a private device, like a camera server on a Private LAN, you use port forwarding. There are some circumstances where that may not be what you want. For example you may have two addresses on the public side of the router. You can only use the primary for port forwarding. If you wanted to use the other address to get into your camera server, you would set up DNAT. Sadly DNAT is a little beyond the scope of this text and will be covered in VOL2.

FIREWALL/NAT GROUPS

The last tab that you see on the Firewall/NAT category is the Firewall/NAT groups option. In this tab you can create a shortcut. You can create these groups which allow you to quickly lump a special category together, and then apply that category to a firewall or a NAT rule. The firewall or the NAT rule is looking for a matching condition, so let's say that you have three networks in your LAN. 192.168.10.0/24, 192.168.20.0/24, and 192.168.30.0/24. Well, here is the starting Point: Create the New Group.

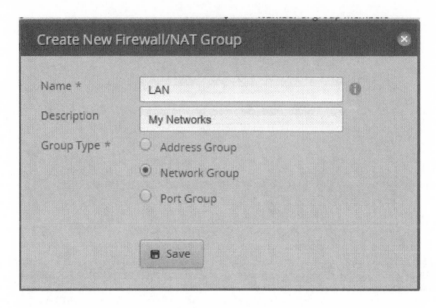

I then navigate to the actions dropdown on the far right and select the config option.

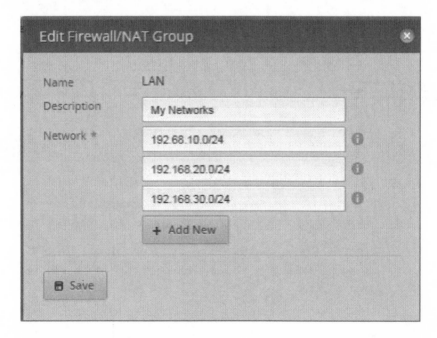

Here, I have added my three Networks. So what the heck do I do with these? Excellent question. This is a very quick way to describe all your LAN devices, so if you are setting up a firewall rule, and you want to allow local traffic to pass to the internet, here is a quick look at that. I have made a Ruleset I called Rule1.

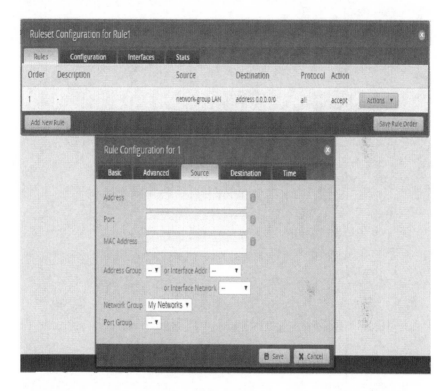

Ok, so the top part that says Ruleset Configuration for Rule1 is looking at the *SOURCE*, traffic of the Network Group I made earlier called My Networks. You don't see it, but on the basic tab I selected the accept button. On the source tab, I have selected the Network Group of My Networks. Let me show you the destination tab.

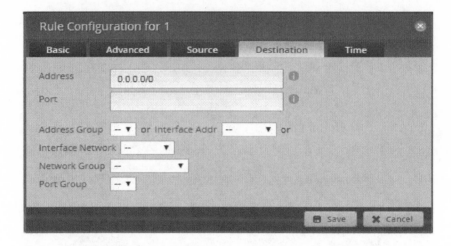

Ok the destination is the address of 0.0.0.0/0. That is the internet, so I do not have to do a huge amount of typing or configuring to allow all the local traffic to get to the internet. This is just an example of the power of the group settings. Now obviously, the real firewall would be loaded with all kinds of rulesets and associated rules. I just showed the basic use of the Group. You can also use groups of addresses, or even ports to make your matches. Like I said, it's like a cool shortcut. Remember, at the back of the book there will be a firewall that you can implement and configure.

I remember setting up one of my first firewalls. I didn't really think that it was too hard. I had gotten bits and pieces from a site on the web. I found out about some rules to prevent viruses, and then I found a few suggestions on Worms, and Trojans too. I was pretty pleased with myself. That is, until I restarted the router. I had forgotten to allow myself into the darn thing. I guess I could have used a little more research. Lesson learned.

Queues first, and then some actual routing. I promise.

Chapter 6

QUEUES

Let's not get crazy. I mean it.

Queues are part of what is commonly known as Quality of Service, or QOS. In the routing and switching world QOS is as complicated as quantum physics, or so it may seem. The router operating system, the code behind the scenes, was developed many years ago and has chugged right along allowing for improvements in many areas. One of them is QOS. What QOS is supposed to do, or allow you to do if you know what you are doing, is to give priority to certain traffic, traffic types, or port usage; cool stuff like that. Now, because there are lots and lots of variables, and lots of different types of traffic, it becomes complex in a hurry.

So Cletus, you have a small network, and on that network you support IP phones, and you have limited bandwidth. One of your goals is to set things up so your phone calls don't get dropped or slowed by other traffic. So, if Uncle Larry is downloading a Linux ISO file, the correct QOS settings will give important bandwidth to the IP phones, and a little less speed for Uncle Larry.

To be able to set this up on a router, prior to version 1.7 in Edge world, you had to create complex sets of rules. These rules are called policies. To *SHAPE* traffic you would use a *SHAPER* policy. Inside the policy you would set up a group of rules that would allow a percentage of available bandwidth and also you would associate a number level priority to that particular port, or traffic type. Oh, also there are other types of policies you can create, not just shaper policies.

Here is an abbreviated *SHAPER* policy. This is done at the CLI.

```
Configure:
set traffic-policy shaper shaper1 bandwidth 100 mbit
```

```
set traffic-policy shaper shaper1 default bandwidth 15%
set traffic-policy shaper shaper1 ceiling 20%
set traffic-policy shaper shaper1 default priority 7
```

setting http traffic*

```
set traffic-policy shaper shaper1 class 2 match port 80
ip source port 80
set traffic-policy shaper shaper1 class 2 bandwidth 20%
set traffic-policy shaper shaper1 class 2 ceiling 100%
set traffic-policy shaper shaper1 class 2 priority 3
```

** ftp traffic***

```
set traffic-policy shaper shaper1 class 3 match port 21
ip source port 21
set traffic-policy shaper shaper1 class 3 match port 20
ip source port 20
set traffic-policy shaper shaper1 class 3 bandwidth 1%
set traffic-policy shaper shaper1 class 3 ceiling 25%
set traffic-policy shaper shaper1 class 3 priority 4
```

http encrypted

```
set traffic-policy shaper shaper1 class 4 match port 443
ip source port 443
set traffic-policy shaper shaper1 class 4 bandwidth 10%
set traffic-policy shaper shaper1 class 4 ceiling 30%
set traffic-policy shaper shaper1 class 4 priority 4
```

Ok, once again let's not get crazy. I am only showing a made up example of how a shaper policy looks. Don't worry about the numbers, concentrate on the insanity.

This is only a little piece of the whole thing. So you can sort of decode a little bit of this by yourself. You see that for each service running on a specific port we can decide the priority, which is a number like 4. We can also specify how much of the actual bandwidth we give that process. The ceiling is a setting on the maximum it could use. The insanity part is that not only is this lots of work, it's also very hard to get perfect. In other words, who is to say that the best setting is priority x, when, maybe it should be priority y? Well Cletus, your day has arrived, and its name is Smart Queue. It's located on the QOS tab.

SMART QUEUE

What sorcery is this? Well this is very, very cool. Here is what this thing does. You basically tell it what ethernet port is used for the WAN, and you tell it how much bandwidth you have, and it will use its internal wizardry to apply priorities. I don't want to get into too much detail about the innards of this utility. It works very well. Let's look at it.

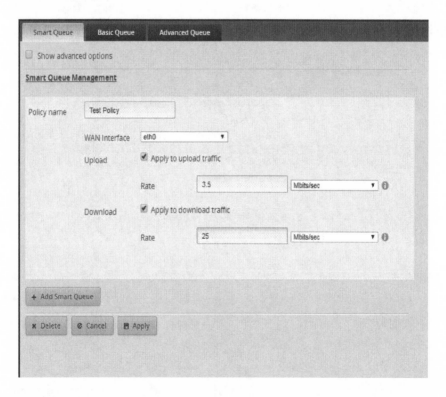

The first thing I did, was to go to ww.speedtest.net and run a speed test on my network. My download speed was listed at around 25, and my upload speed was 3.5 Mbps. You can see that those are the numbers I have plugged in. I also have to select the port of eth0 as my connection to the internet. All you have to do is click apply. That is it, you are done. Now if you do another speed test, you will find that the numbers are going to be less than they were the first time. You might say, "Hey this thing is eating up my Bandwidth," and you would sort of be correct. You see, if you see less speed on your next speed test, then you know it's actually working the way you want it to work. What it's doing is creating a buffer or unusable bandwidth in case you really need it for that speed sensitive IP phone. Below you can see some traffic flows. Some are fat, some are skinny. IP Phones traffic is skinny. If the Smart Queue senses that the IP phone flow is getting too restricted, it will borrow from the Fat flow; the ISO download. You don't need to know how all this works behind the curtain. It works very well, and you get the added bonus of not having to be an internet traffic engineer.

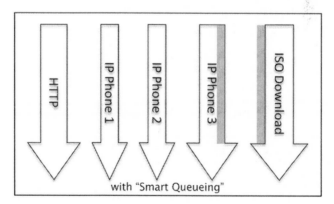

You may have noticed by now that I have not had you open the *SHOW ADVANCED OPTION BOX.* So, go ahead and open that up. Let's see what we have. I am only showing the upload portion of the window, as both the Upload and the Download sections show the same selections.

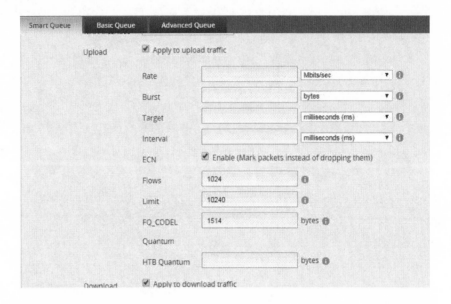

These settings are for the use of what is known as *BURSTING*. Bursting is generally used for slow speed connections, so if you are on a very slow WAN connection, bursting can be used. The effects of bursting are rather positive. They allow a user to load a web page faster, and generally have a little smoother web experience. The real nuts and bolts of bursting are beyond the scope of this book, but I do want to give you some direction.

Bursting is like you sitting in your car creeping along a busy freeway at 35 MPH. The first thing you see is a rate setting. That's how fast we can possibly go. For the download at my house, it's 25 Mbit per second. For the freeway we have 70 MPH. The burst setting is measured in bytes, and that is how much data you can grab at the full rate.

For your car, I will let you go 70 MPH for one mile. The target number is a measurement of queue delay, and the interval number has to do with dropping of packets. The cool thing is that both the target and the interval number will be automatically set for slow connections. Don't worry about the mechanics of this. Clearly these settings are not for the beginner. There is plenty of information out there on the web for those who want to get more information. One important thing about bursting; it should be used for slow WAN connections. Please do a little research before you set this thing up.

There are some people out there who use the Smart Queue to control the speed of a connection. Yes, you could put different numbers in here. I could have put the download speed of 5 Mbit per second rather than 25, and that would indeed slow things down. Do not do that. The Smart Queue would think that you need less overall bandwidth to play with so of course this would change your speeds. I have also seen people who change the interface configuration of a port to modify speed by changing the Speed/Duplex setting. As shown below. This is not the right way to limit speed to or from your network. Nope.

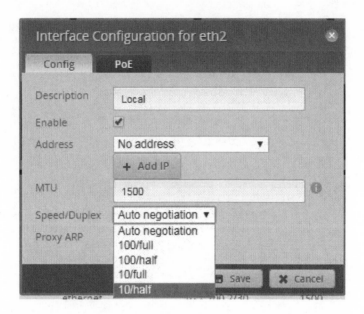

Don't set the Speed/Duplex setting wrong on purpose. If you do not know what to set it to, leave it on Auto negotiation. Now let's review.

Use Smart Queue by selecting the actual upload and download numbers.

Do not use this utility, or the Interface config utility to fiddle with speed.

If some super-duper router configuration expert has already gone through your router, and has created Shaper policies, then you should not use the Smart Queue, as these settings are not compatible; like me and broccoli.

You can go to the config tree and select traffic policy, expand the + button, and oh my, there are no less than nine different policies here. If somebody has created a policy previously, you will see it here. Like I said, policies that are created are in direct conflict with the SMART QUEUE. If you try to run both at the same time, your router will run like a sloth, and while sloths are cool to look at, they are just not reliable in the packet delivery world.

So, if you really want to control traffic speed to or from someone, or an entire network, let's look at BASIC QUEUE.

BASIC QUEUE

This is the spot for all of you speed controlling freaks.

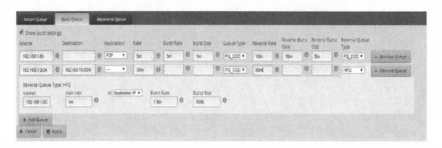

Instead of dragging you through the setup, I have already configured a Basic Queue, and I will describe what it is doing. This is the place to set Bandwidth Restrictions.

I have made two separate queues. The first is for a specific device with the address of 192.168.1.65, and that is under the *SOURCE*, so the source of the traffic is 192.168.1.65.

I have left the destination box blank, and in this router, that means all destinations, so the source of 192.168.1.65 to anywhere, and the application I have selected is PtP (Peer to Peer). The way the router knows how to identify that type of traffic is through the Traffic Analysis tab, so jump over there real fast and select the *ENABLE* button next to Operational Status. This will allow the router to understand the traffic type.

Ok, sorry, we got sidetracked. This device is also allowed to burst up to the speed of 3mbit per second to get one meg of data. The queue type is *FQ_CODEL*. Now, the reverse rate is just that; traffic *COMING BACK* to the address of 192.168.1.65.

I want you to think of your queue as cars on one lane of the freeway. A freeway where all the lanes will converge down to one lane only. Other cars are being added all the time. If we end up with too many cars in the lane trying to get into the lane or *QUEUE*, then we have a problem. In the case of *FQ_CODEL* we have each lane of the freeway, or each traffic flow being accessed equally; hence the term *FAIRNESS*. In other words, all the cars are taking turns equally merging into the one lane.

There is also the selection of *PFIFO*, or *PRIORITY FIRST IN FIRST OUT*. The traffic will be lined up in our Queue by the priority assigned to it. In other words, that VOIP packet will have priority over a plain Jane data packet.

Next, we have *HFQ* or *HOST FAIRNESS QUEUING*. This is designed for a single host. *HFQ* is used when all the hosts on a network will share the same policy.

Then we have *SFQ*, or *STOCHASTIC FAIRNESS QUEUING*. Where traffic is separated into multiple First in First out queues and then serviced in a *ROUND ROBIN* format.

Ok, now that you are totally confused, let's see what I have set up here. Let's go back to the first line. Breaking it down, we have one device that can upload data at the rate of 5 mbps. He can download, or reverse rate at 10 mbps. He can also burst upload to 3 mbps to get 1 mbps of data. The reverse burst, or download side is telling us that this device can burst at 15 mbps to accumulate 5 mbps of data.

We are using the *FAIR QUEUE* with *CODEL* in each direction. This is a very normal setup. Now, the second line is showing an entire subnet; 192.168.1.0/24 which represents the capability to have up to 254 devices. These settings apply to each device separately. The entire network, cumulatively, has 30 mbps upload and 60 mbps download, and since I want the same policy to affect everyone on the LAN, I have set up *HFQ* for my download or reverse side. What happens when you select *HFQ* you get that additional *REVERSE QUEUE TYPE* area.

You will have to enter the ID, which in our case is destination IP. That refers to our LAN. From the direction of the LAN of 192.168.10.0 going to our LAN of 192.168.1.0 we are limiting the download speed to 1 mbps. We can burst at 1.5 mbps to get 500k of data.

That is how limiting bandwidth should be done. Once again there are several options that I am not covering here, but I think you have some understanding to move ahead from here.

You can add as many of these *BASIC QUEUES* as you please. You can limit upload, and download traffic based on traffic types, like P2P, or all traffic.

The last bit of advice here is test, test, test. Start simple and then get complex, not the other way around. One of the best ways to test something is with two routers. Set up a simple network for each side. Then, once you have set up a route between them, you can fool with the settings on the BASIC QUEUE TAB and see the result. Lucky for us, the next chapter will show us how to set up routing.

I know that you will also see an ADVANCED QUEUE TAB next to the Basic Queue. This feature will not be covered in this text, but will be covered in Vol2.

Chapter 7

ROUTING

Let us go back to the very beginning of this book where I spoke of the things you will need to get your router setup and on online. You need a valid LAN side address. You need a WAN address. You need NAT to get from the inside to the outside and you need DNS to resolve web sites into IP addresses. Then we need a way out and a way in; a route. The real cool part here is that if you set up everything else, the router is smart enough to know that there is only one way out. It will see the settings for NAT, and once it senses a connection on that port, you will be able to move traffic.

Let's cover the process of routing. The idea is to move packets from your network to another network, whether that's the ISP or a different network. To do this, there are some rules that we must be aware of. One of those rules deals with route selection. You see, there are going to be situations where there is more than one path to get to the intended destination. One of the many things that the router will look at is something called *ADMINISTRATIVE DISTANCE*. This is a universal measurement amongst routers. Administrative Distance is a way to rank, or weigh the best route. Sometimes this is referred to as a measurement of cost. Here, the lowest value will always be the selected route.

I know that sounds a little strange but hang in there. We are going to be setting up a static route first. By default, static routes have an *ADMINISTRATIVE DISTANCE* of one. If we were to physically connect two routers together with an ethernet cable, both devices would be able to route data, and the AD would be the lowest number; 0. These routes are considered to be directly connected. A direct connection is an AD of 0. The lowest number being a reflection of how trustworthy the route is. Well, if we have a cable connecting the two devices, then I would consider that connection very reliable.

When we set up a static route, we need to know two key pieces of information. We need the *DESTINATION NETWORK ADDRESS*, and we need to know the address of the gateway. The destination is the network that contains the host, or the server that we are trying to reach. The gateway is the router that knows how to get to this destination network.

Ok, I did say that routers do the heavy lifting of getting data from here to there. There is another factor that this device will consider in that process. It has to do with how much info that the router has. Consider the following destinations:

Destination Address:

1. 192.168.10.0/24 via gateway of 5.1.1.1

2. 192.168.0.0/16 via gateway of 5.1.1.2

3. 192.168.10.0/28 via gateway of 5.1.1.3

I know this looks easy. There are three routes to get to where we want to go. Which one of these would the Router select? Well, it would select the third choice. You see the mask, or the CIDR notation of /28? Well, the longer the mask, the more specific the destination becomes. All these routes would eventually get you there, but the most effective is the third one. To prove my theory let's look at a routing table from Microsoft Windows, and break it down.

I am only showing the IPv4 side of this, but here we can see how a client computer sees the world. My PC has an address of 192.168.1.107. I can see everything from 192.168.1.1 all the way up to 192.168.1.254. If my PC had a packet it wanted to send to anything in that range, it would know to send out a broadcast message to find that client.

Remember what DNS does? Let's say I open a browser and type in the address www.Cat.com. Behind the scenes, a DNS server will return an address of something like 2.99.5.2 to my PC. My PC will then look in the routing table to see if that address is known, or listed, here. As you can see, it is not. So, what does my PC do with that packet? I will give you a hint, the closest address to 2.99.5.2 is 0.0.0.0. You see, the zeros are just a variable, meaning any number. So, if there is no match locally to the 192.168.1.0 network, then the packet is forwarded to the gateway. Just as it is listed there at the top. The Gateway is 192.168.1.1. That is the way, or route, to the website www.cat.com.

By the way, the website has nothing to do with cats. What a disappointment. Anyway, you could set a static route to the internet, a *DEFAULT ROUTE* with a destination address of 0.0.0.0/0. That would work. Again, the zeros mean that it would match every destination, so let's look at how to set a static route in the router. Basic Drawing number 2 first.

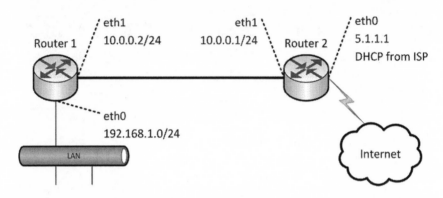

Here we have two routers and each one is connected to a network that connects the two together. We shall pretend that Router 1 is connected to the Sales department in a remote building, and has a local address of 192.168.1.0/24. Router 2 is connected to the internet with the router getting a DHCP internet address of 5.1.1.1 at eth0 of Router 2.

This is actually the way my home network is currently set up. I have a PC on my LAN of 192.168.1.0/24 to get onto the internet. I will make a static route from Router 1 to the network I am trying to get to on Router 2. That network is going to be 0.0.0.0/0.

Open the Routing Tab, and select the option to *ADD STATIC ROUTE*. It should look like this:

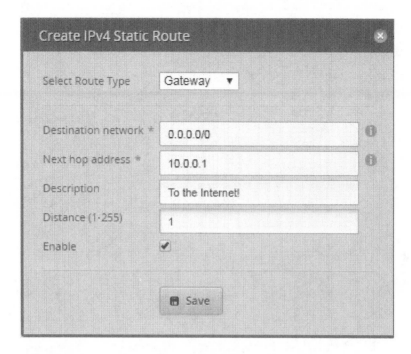

And when you look at the Dashboard you see this:

My local address is on eth0 and it's the 192.168.1.0/24 network. The Eth1 network is 10.0.0.2. Ok, I really need you to understand this part. The next hop address (gateway) for my PC, (look at the drawing), is 10.0.0.1. In the world of static routing that will never change. If there was a Router 3 out there, past Router 2, my next hop is always going to be 10.0.0.1. That's the gateway so this will work the same way in reverse. If there was a LAN on Router 2 and they wanted to access something on the LAN for Router 1, then they would have to make a static route on Router 2.

Ok I have made a change to our Drawing. Let's look.

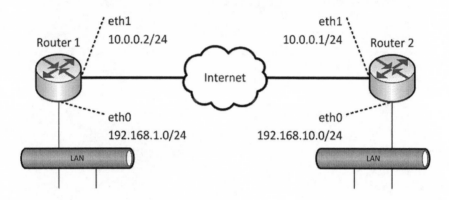

On this version the internet is between the two routers, so we are presuming that the ISP has given us an address for the WAN sides of our routers. I know that looks strange, but consider this: if we use the same ISP for both sides, then the WAN interfaces will be in that provider's network. All we have to do is to get updated gateway addresses from the provider.

In this example I left them as they were before, only this time the destination network will be different. For Router 1 the destination is 192.168.10.0/24. And for Router 2 the destination will be 192.168.1.0/24. The next hop for Router 2 is 10.0.0.2, and the next hop for Router 1 is 10.0.0.1.

Static Routing is easy to set up in the Edge Router. You need to know where you are going, and how you are getting there. The Destination Network is where we are going, and the Gateway Address is how we are getting there.

Also, do not forget how the NAT entry would look. In the picture below, you can see what it is for Router 1. I have left off the bottom of the screen shot, as there is nothing to configure there. All you need to do NAT is know what interface is connected to the WAN side of things, and what method you are using for the translation. In this case I choose to use Masquerade. If you refer to the above drawing you will see that the Eth1 interface is the way to the internet and that applies to both of the above scenarios.

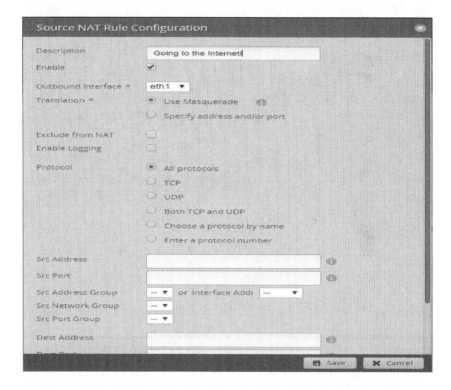

Before we move on to the Dynamic Routing portion, I want to talk about the routing table. This table will display your routes, along with some codes, or attributes, that you should know.

Once you have done all this fun static routing, on the router, in the upper right corner, next to Toolbox, select CLI. This will open the command line. An alternate way to do this would be to use putty to open the CLI. Once there you will need to log in to the router. Enter the Username and password here. Then, at the CLI you will type the command `show ip route`. Hit enter after that and, if done correctly, this is what you will see:

Okie-dokie, you see under the area marked Codes that there is; K for kernel, C for Connected, and S for Static, etc. You will see the static route that you created here, right there at the bottom.

You also see the *> next to it. Well those guys are codes as well. The * means that the route is in the FIB, or the Forwarding Information Base (Routing Table). The > means that is has been selected as the route of choice. In this case it is selected because there is no other route available. I did mention Static, but what about the Code *CONNECTED*? A connected route is one that the router understands because there is a physical cable to that destination. Hence the term connected.

You also see this entry in the Routing Tab under Routes. You can see all the types right there: Static, Connected, Rip, and OSPF. When we get done setting up some OSPF we will return to the CLI and look at the routing table again.

A little review here; a static route is manually set up, and if any of the information were to change, the route would fail. The static route option is best when your network(s) are under your control and rather small. When your network becomes more complex, or just larger, then it's time to move to OSPF.

OSPF: This routing protocol is dynamic, meaning that it will automatically trade information with other routers on the current *STATE* of the links that bind everything together. OSPF is known as a *LINK STATE* routing protocol. Since this protocol is dynamic it can also determine the best path to send data along to another network. Remember that we talked about cost before. OSPF takes that to a little more advanced level. It uses the routing metric of Cost/Delay. What that means is that it uses both an AD (Administrative Distance) number, and a related cost, for each link. The AD number for OSPF is fixed at 110, so it will rely on the cost. It can look at the speed of the lines between the routers, and will always select the fastest connection. Another great thing about OSPF is that if somehow a path becomes unreachable, or disconnected, it can adjust its routing table to find the next best way to get to its destination. That is, if there is more than one way to get where it wants to go.

OSPF stands for *OPEN SHORTEST PATH FIRST*, and that's a great way to describe what it does. I don't want to spend a huge amount of time describing all the nuts and bolts that form the basis of OSPF, but there are some things that you should know.

LINK STATE

OSPF is known as a *LINK STATE* protocol. Basic communication starts when one router, let's say Router A, is configured with OSPF the same way that Router B is, and we have Router A sending out what is known as a *HELLO* packet. The Hello Packet is the first part of the process. The second part of the process is the sending out an advertisement of the links that Router 1 is using. This is called an *LSA*, or Link State Advertisement. Basically, Router 1 would be saying, "Hi there, I am Router 1 and I am connected to two links. One is 192.168.1.0/24, and one is 10.0.0.0/24."

This LSA is sent out all OSPF interfaces, so Router 2 is going to go through the same process; "Hello, here are the Links or networks that I am connected to, so add them your database."

This database is called the LSD, or Link State Database. Now the last part of this tango is, once all the routers know who their neighbors are, and what networks they are connected to, they will calculate the routes to find out the best way to get from one network to another. This is called the Dijkstra algorithm. I don't want to go into all the parameters of the algorithm, but it will help the routers do all the calculations to find out which path to take to all the networks. The benefit of this setup is the ability to have some fault tolerance built in. This means that if one link should fail, every device in the database will know about that failure. They will go through the same process again, and will end up with a new routing table that will direct them around that failed link.

Terminology update, the term is *CONVERGENCE*. This is when all the routers agree on the correctness of the entries in the LSD. OSPF *CONVERGES* very fast. If a link should become unplugged, or just outright fail, all the routers that are participating in this database know about it and can *DYNAMICALLY* come up with a new route table. Cool.

AREAS

An OSPF area is designed to organize, or group, OSPF routers into a configurable division. This division could be geographic, or function based. At the top of the whole shebang we have what is called an Autonomous System, or AS. An AS is a group of routers that are controlled or owned by a single entity. Sort of like all the routers for a large company. When the number of routers in that company becomes too large, it can be broken up into smaller groups, and those are *AREAS*.

BACKBONE

The *BACKBONE* is the first Area. Yup, the very first Area is called the Backbone, and if you have a small OSPF network, all your routers can be a member of the Area called Backbone. This is the first area, so it follows that all routes and additional added areas will have a path back to the backbone. The Area ID for the backbone is 0.0.0.0. I know that it looks like an IP address, but it's not.

Here is some of the clever stuff about OSPF and Areas; when all these devices are saying hello, and they are building routes, and doing route calculations, they are only sharing that data with devices in their own area. If they need to send something to another area, that is, if your network is that big, they will forward packets to a router that connects to another area. That device has one foot in both areas, and is called an *AREA BORDER ROUTER*, or ABR. The idea is to partition the network so that all this information is kept to a manageable size, and our routers don't crush the CPU doing all those calculations. A smaller database equals faster throughput speeds for all our devices.

What I want to do here is start with a clean setup. Let's look at a simple network diagram:

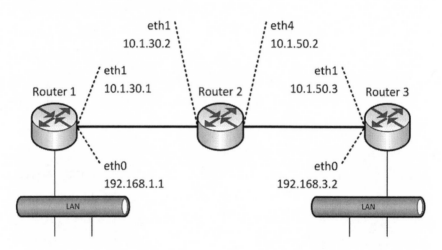

Here we have three routers. If we had just two then static routing would be fine right? We have Router 1, Router 2, and Router 3. Router 1 has a LAN of 192.168.1.1, and on eth1 we have 10.1.30.1 so we are going to configure OSPF in the CLI of the routers. We will see the result in the GUI when we are done.

Just a few things before we get going. The CLI has two modes. There is Operational Mode, which is indicated by a $ at the prompt.

At this mode there are basic commands to view the configuration. Basically, you are going to make all changes at the next mode, called the Configuration mode. This is indicated by a # sign at the prompt. You have to log in first, using your username and password, and you will go into Configuration Mode by typing: $configure. Let's see the entries for each router in this scenario. To get from $ to #, you will type: configure, and then hit enter.

Ok, let's look at the damage. We have set the Router ID, a 32-bit number assigned to each router running the OSPF protocol. This number uniquely identifies the router within an *AUTONOMOUS SYSTEM*. We will do that for all three routers. The next line identifies the area as the backbone. After that we have manually entered the cost, the hello and dead intervals. Hello is what starts off the conversation. The dead timer is how long another router will wait to hear from you before it considers the link to be dead, or down. If the dead timer reaches zero, then everyone has to build routes all over again. The retransmission interval is just that. It will specify the amount of time between LSA's. Transmit delay configures the transmit delay for link- update packets, which is the estimated time required for OSPF to send link-state update packets on the interface to which you are connected. We get to do that for all the routers.

```
cletus@R1#set interfaces ethernet eth1 address
10.1.30.1/24
```

This will set the address on the interface eth1.

```
cletus@R1#set protocols ospf parameters router-id
10.0.50.1
cletus@R1#set protocols ospf area 0.0.0.0 network
10.0.50.0/24
cletus@R1#set interfaces ethernet eth1 ip ospf cost 10
```

```
cletus@R1#set interfaces ethernet eth1 ip ospf dead-
interval 40
cletus@R1#set interfaces ethernet eth1 ip ospf hello-
interval 10
cletus@R1#set interfaces ethernet eth1 ip ospf priority 1
cletus@R1#set interfaces ethernet eth1 ip ospf
retransmit-interval 5
cletus@R1#set interfaces ethernet eth1 ip ospf transmit-
delay 1
```

Configure the IP addresses:

```
Cletus@R2#set interfaces ethernet eth1 address 10.1.30.2
Cletus@R2#set interfaces ethernet eth4 address 10.1.50.2
```

Configure OSPF:

```
Cletus@R2#set protocols ospf parameters router-id
10.1.30.1
Cletus@R2#set protocols ospf area 0.0.0.0 network
10.1.30.0/24
Cletus@R2#set protocols ospf area 0.0.0.0 network
10.1.50.0/24
Cletus@R2#set interfaces ethernet eth1 ip ospf cost 10
Cletus@R2#set interfaces ethernet eth1 ip ospf dead-
interval 40
Cletus@R2#set interfaces ethernet eth1 ip ospf hello-
interval 10
Cletus@R2#set interfaces ethernet eth1 ip ospf priority 1
Cletus@R2#set interfaces ethernet eth1 ip ospf
retransmit-interval 5
Cletus@R2#set interfaces ethernet eth1 ip ospf transmit-
delay 1
Cletus@R2#set interfaces ethernet eth4 ip ospf cost 10
Cletus@R2#set interfaces ethernet eth4 ip ospf dead-
interval 40
Cletus@R2#set interfaces ethernet eth4 ip ospf hello-
interval 10
Cletus@R2#set interfaces ethernet eth4 ip ospf priority 1
Cletus@R2#set interfaces ethernet eth4 ip ospf
retransmit-interval 5
Cletus@R2#set interfaces ethernet eth4 ip ospf transmit-
delay 1
```

Just one more Router to set up!

Configure the IP address:

```
Cletus@R3#set interfaces ethernet eth0 address 10.1.50.3
```

Configure OSPF:

```
Cletus@R3#set protocols ospf parameters router-id
10.1.50.3
Cletus@R3#set protocols ospf area 0.0.0.0 network
10.1.50.0/24
Cletus@R3#set interfaces ethernet eth0 ip ospf cost 10
Cletus@R3#set interfaces ethernet eth0 ip ospf dead-
interval 40
Cletus@R3#set interfaces ethernet eth0 ip ospf hello-
interval 10
Cletus@R3#set interfaces ethernet eth0 ip ospf priority 1
Cletus@R3#set interfaces ethernet eth0 ip ospf
retransmit-interval 5
Cletus@R3#set interfaces ethernet eth0 ip ospf transmit-
delay 1
```

Okie dokie. Once this is configured, R1 learns that 10.1.50.0/24 can be reached by 10.1.30.2:

```
Cletus@R1:~$ show ip route Codes: K - kernel route, C -
connected, S -static, R - RIP, O – OSPF, I - ISIS, B -
BGP, > - selected route, * - FIB route

S>* 0.0.0.0/0 [210/0] via 192.168.1.1, eth5
O 10.1.30.0/24 [110/10] is directly connected, eth1,
00:00:27
C>* 10.1.30.0/24 is directly connected, eth1
O>* 10.1.50.0/24 [110/20] via 10.0.50.2, eth1, 00:00:11
C>* 127.0.0.0/8 is directly connected, lo
C>* 172.16.6.0/24 is directly connected,eth2
```

You will now be able to ping all the way from one side to the other. You can do a Traceroute as well. The Router1 interface will look like this.

There you have it. Not really that complicated, but very important. There are other OSPF commands that you can use.

```
Cletus@R1:~$ show ip ospf
Cletus@R1:~$ show ip ospf database
```

Just a little more information on OSPF. The nature of this routing protocol is Link State. Think about that. The actual link is really the Ethernet cable being present and happy. If the cable were to become broken or unplugged the state of the connection had indeed changed. The act of convergence where all the routers have all the updated routing table info is very fast with this protocol.

Routing protocols route traffic in the form of TCP, or UDP.

Chapter 8

VPN

What is a VPN and why do we want them? In short, it's a Virtual Private Network. That network is a very clever and secure way to connect devices and entire networks together. The largest WAN in the world is the Internet. When we move data, in the form of packets, let's say, from our house to our workplace, we are going across the very open and very non-secure internet. The idea is to be able to move our packets safely and securely, so nobody can intercept or otherwise fiddle about with our data. You may also see the term *TUNNEL*. That term describes how the traffic is moving.

In a VPN, the traffic is *TUNNELED* through another network, whether it is just tunneling through an internal network, or going out over the Internet. We are going to examine two types of tunnels. We will look at both PPTP, and L2TP.

PPTP

Does anyone remember the Bat Phone? Yes the Bat Phone. Batman would pick it up and it was directly connected to Police Commissioner Gordon's office. If you imagine a phone that only has one place to connect to or from, then you can picture a VPN.

The first VPN we want to examine is the PPTP VPN. Many people feel that this protocol is outdated, and should not be used, due to it having several security issues. Apple devices running OS-10 will not support this VPN protocol. If you are going to be supporting Apple devices, this will not be the Protocol you want to employ.

It can still be configured very quickly and easily in the Edge Router. Clearly you will have to decide about the level of security that you *NEED* for your connections. I am going to walk you through a basic setup of the PPTP VPN. Let's look at that screen. Navigate to the VPN tab.

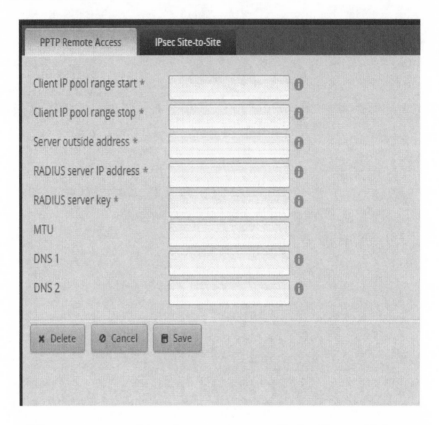

When you open this tab, you can see all the fun stuff that you need to tell the router in order to set up PPTP. You need a range of IP addresses to allocate to the clients that are connecting to your network. You need the *OUTSIDE* address of the server. That is the Public address on your router. The address that is on the Internet side. To find the Public IP, you can type "What is my IP" in a browser window.

You also see here that you are required to enter the Radius Server's address and Server Key. Ok, what the heck is Radius? Radius is a security service that performs authentication, among other things. It runs on a separate server. In some cases, Radius can be run on advanced routers, but it's most often run on a server. There are many flavors of Radius designed and built for Open Source, or for proprietary operating systems. For our purposes, we will not be using Radius. Since Radius performs authentication, we will have our router handle that task.

In our GUI window there is no option for allowing the router to perform authentication. You can't use every feature of the router in the GUI. For some setup stuff we need to get to the CLI. Let's go to the CLI. I used Putty to go to the CLI, but you can do this either way.

```
login as: Cletus

Welcome to EdgeOs

Cletus@ubnt:~$ configure

[edit]

Cletus@ubnt# set vpn pptp remote-access authentication
mode local

[edit]

Cletus@ubnt# set vpn pptp remote-access authentication
local-users username Cletus password ubnt

[edit]

Cletus@ubnt# set vpn pptp remote-access authentication
local-users username paul password dingo

Cletus@ubnt# set vpn pptp remote-access client-ip-pool
start 192.168.1.250
```

```
[edit]

Cletus@ubnt# set vpn pptp remote-access client-ip-pool
stop 192.168.1.254

[edit

Cletus@ubnt# set vpn pptp remote-access outside-address
119.10.1.1

[edit]

Cletus@ubnt# set vpn pptp remote-access dns-servers
server-1 8.8.8.8

[edit]

Cletus@ubnt# set vpn pptp remote-access dns-servers
server-2 4.2.2.1

[edit]

Cletus@ubnt# set firewall name WAN_LOCAL rule 30 action
accept

[edit]

Cletus@ubnt# set firewall name WAN_LOCAL rule 30
description Allow_PPTP

[edit]

Cletus@ubnt# set firewall name WAN_LOCAL rule 30
destination port 1723

[edit]

Cletus@ubnt# set firewall name WAN_LOCAL rule 30 log
disable

[edit]

Cletus@ubnt# set firewall name WAN_LOCAL rule 30
protocol tcp

[edit]

Cletus@ubnt# set firewall name WAN_LOCAL rule 40 action
accept
```

```
[edit]

Cletus@ubnt# set firewall name WAN_LOCAL rule 40
description allow_pptp_gre

[edit]

Cletus@ubnt# set firewall name WAN_LOCAL rule 40
protocol gre

[edit]

Cletus@ubnt# set firewall name WAN_LOCAL rule 40 log
disable

[edit]

Cletus@ubnt# commit

[ vpn ]

Restarting PPTP:

Stopping PPTP: pptpd.

Starting PPTP Daemon: pptpd.

[edit]

Cletus@ubnt# save
```

OK, what did we just do? As you read from the top, you can see we have our Authentication setup as Local. This means that the router will create the users Cletus, and Paul. It also sets the passwords for those users.

Next, we have our DHCP Pool of addresses ready to go. After that we show the Outside Address. Remember that is the one that is on the public side of our router. It is shown as 119. 10.1.1. Of course, yours will be different.

Then we have the commands for the DNS server address that we want our clients to use. Then at last we are setting a couple of rules in our Firewall.

You may notice that I have used them as Rule 30, and 40. The reason I did that is that I may want to cram other rules in before these, and I may want to insert rules between these two.

The first rule is allowing PPTP to arrive on the destination port of 1723. The second rule is allowing the protocol GRE. Then, it's just commit and save. Remember that commit is saving everything to the active configuration. Save is used to copy all that to the startup configuration of the device. When the router does a reboot, it will have all that config ready to go.

Now go into the GUI, and look at the VPN tab. You will see on the VPN Tab, all the settings that you put into the CLI. What is missing is the Radius portion. We are not using Radius Authentication for this setup. We are using Local mode. Our local users are Cletus and Paul, and we already dynamically assigned them passwords as well.

The screen shows you that this was configured by a CLI or a Config Tree setup, and if you wanted to use this GUI to set anything up, you would have to go back to the CLI or Config Tree and delete everything.

PPTP Remote Access	IPsec Site-to-Site

PPTP VPN was configured using the CLI or Config Tree on UI. Using this form to configu
must disable those changes before using this form.

Client IP pool range start *	**192.168.1.250**
Client IP pool range stop *	**192.168.1.254**
Server outside address *	**119.10.1.1**
RADIUS server IP address *	
RADIUS server key *	
MTU	1492
DNS 1	8.8.8.8
DNS 2	4.2.2.1

If you want to change anything, you want to open Config Tree. Once there you can navigate to VPN. It will be toward the bottom. Notice that it is now in **Bold**. As you open VPN, then PPTP, you just keep following the highlighted areas until you find what you want to change. So if you wanted to change the Password for the user Paul, then open, Remote-Access, Authentication, Local-Users, Username, Paul. Here you will find the box for Password. The Config Tree is a great tool.

Notice in the above screen the readout for MTU. That stands for Maximum Transmission Unit. In regular Ethernet the MTU is 1500. That means that each packet is 1500 bytes. You see here that the size for our VPN is 1492. You will also see other MTU sizes used in Edge Devices. Changing the MTU to a smaller number actually helps out some of the inherent problems with things like path discovery. You can see this as an option in the TCP MSS clamping wizard. So, 1492 is a completely normal setting. It is extremely helpful that the VPN setup does this for us.

DYN DNS

I want to insert a short discussion on Dynamic DNS. Let's all go back to when I described that your WAN address as a Public address. It's an address that is reachable from the Internet. Sometimes that outside or public address may change. Your service provider does not always let you keep the same address. If that happens, your VPN will fail because of that address change. To avoid that problem, the Edge router supports Dynamic DNS. It relies on a web-based service company to map a name to your IP address. It will keep track of any changes that the service provider performs, and *DYNAMICALLY* map the new IP address to the same name. Very cool. There are several dynamic services out there that you can use. Of course, if you are creating a VPN that goes through a corporate network where you control IP addresses, there would be no need for Dynamic DNS.

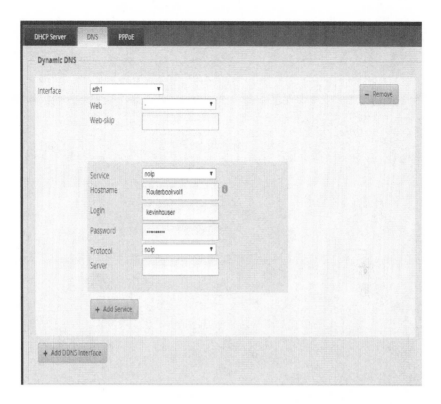

Here we see the entries for the service *NoIP*. You can navigate to www.noip.com on the Internet, set up an account (it's free), and once you have a Hostname setup, and a Login and Password, you just transfer that info to this section of the DNS Tab. If you look at the above Hostname, you will see that if I was to actually finish the online setup, I would be able to access my network from home by opening a browser and going to Routerbookvol1.noip.com But on the client side I would have to know those names and Passwords that I set up on the VPN itself. That means I would log in as Paul or Cletus with the correct password. I would not use the login that is listed above; Kevinhouser, that is the login for the router to talk to the server at the website www.noip.com. It would seem that everybody has their favorite service to do this function. Once again I do not represent NOIP, nor do I make anything from using them as an example. Do the research and find the one service that you feel comfortable with. Ok, remember that if you wanted to access something like a camera server, you will still have to set up Port Forwarding.

L2TP

Layer 2 Tunneling Protocol.

Here are the nuts and bolts of L2TP. There are a few terms that you should understand before we get into the configuration. First, the L2TP protocol, all by itself does not provide encryption of data, nor does it provide for *DATA INTEGRITY*. Data integrity is a way to make sure that nothing from the sender has been changed or altered in any way. *ENCRYPTION* is a way to turn plain text into cipher text, that is, something unreadable. Also, *AUTHENTICATION* is a way to prove that you are who you claim to be. Something like using a name and password combination, or a fingerprint scan.

When setting up security for the L2TP VPN there are two choices for security; Pre-shared Key and EAP which uses certificates. A certificate is something that is issued by a Certificate Authority and is used for authentication. Think about your Driver's license. It's a certificate in a way. It's issued by a trusted authority; the DMV. So when the nice officer wants to see it while you are pulled over on the side of the road, he/she can be sure that the information on that license is valid.

A pre-shared key is basically a password that each side already knows before they make the connection. It's what you use to connect to your Wifi. Others may not know the password to access the network, and that helps to make it secure. When we set up our L2TP connection we use a Pre-Shared key. We will also use the router to authenticate our VPN clients. Let's look at a typical setup.

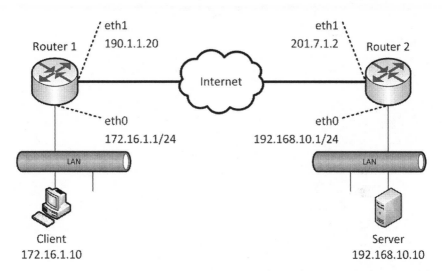

Here we have a client PC on the left connected to Router 1, and we have a server on the right connected to Router 2. We are going to configure Router 2. We want an L2TP connection from the client to the server. We are going to assume that the Router 2 has been configured with a Basic Setup Wizard so the devices inside the LAN have NAT setup, so they know the way to the Internet.

The first thing we do is run everything from the CLI. The first step is logging in and going to configure mode. Then we set up the wan interface, and the internal network information.

```
Cletus@ubnt:~$ configure

[edit]

Cletus@ubnt# set vpn ipsec ipsec-interfaces interface
eth4

[edit]
```

```
Cletus@ubnt# set vpn ipsec nat-networks allowed-network
192.168.10.1/24

[edit]

Cletus@ubnt# set vpn ipsec nat-traversal enable

[edit]

Cletus@ubnt# set vpn l2tp remote-access authentication
mode local

[edit]

Cletus@ubnt# set vpn l2tp remote-access authentication
local-users username Cletus password ubnt

[edit]

Cletus@ubnt# set vpn l2tp remote-access client-ip-pool
start 192.168.10.240

[edit]

Cletus@ubnt# set vpn l2tp remote-access client-ip-pool
stop 192.168.10.250

[edit]
```

Ok, let's go over this part before we finish the rest. The first part is where you are telling the router which interface is the WAN interface. In my case it's Eth4.

The next part tells the VPN which networks they can reach. In my case it's the 192.168.10.1 network.

Next is Nat Traversal. This allows us to maintain a connection. Don't worry too much about that detail for now, other than to know we need it set up.

After that we have our authentication mode set as local. This will allow the router to do the authentication rather than a Radius Server.

We next have our user who is getting the access, and the password for that user. And finally we have a small pool of IP addresses to assign those connections.

Now we will finish up this portion:

```
Cletus@ubnt# set vpn l2tp remote-access dns-servers
server-1 8.8.8.8

[edit]

Cletus@ubnt# set vpn l2tp remote-access dns-servers
server-2 4.2.2.2

[edit]

Cletus@ubnt# set vpn l2tp remote-access ipsec-settings
authentication mode pre-shared-secret

[edit]

Cletus@ubnt# set vpn l2tp remote-access ipsec-settings
authentication pre-shared-secret Cletusisnumber1

Cletus@ubnt# set vpn l2tp remote-access ipsec-settings
ike-lifetime 3600

[edit]

Cletus@ubnt# set vpn l2tp remote-access outside-address
201.7.1.2

[edit]

Cletus@ubnt# commit
```

There may be a few things different for your setup. If your Internet connection is not static and is getting a DHCP address from the provider, then the outside address part should be set like this:

Set vpn l2tp remote-access dhcp-interface eth4.

Alrighty then. The last part of this puzzle is actually pretty easy. You're going to need to do a little work in the Firewall to allow these L2TP connections to be successful. We are going to create 4 new rules.

Since I used the Basic Setup Wizard, I already have two entries here for the rulesets. I have WAN_IN, and I have WAN_LOCAL. Rules for IN protect the router, and the LOCAL rules are there to protect the users. We are going to add 4 new rules to the WAN_LOCAL ruleset.

Select the Actions dropdown across from WAN_LOCAL and you will see this.

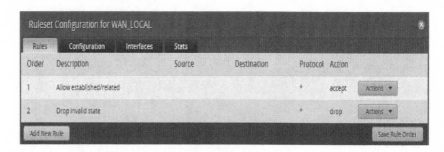

Click Add New Rule. You will see this.

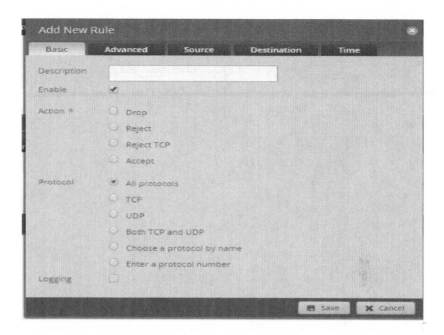

Under Description, enter Allow IKE for VPN, then select accept.

Under the protocol section select UDP.

Once that is done you can click on the destination Tab, and put in the destination port as 500. Like this:

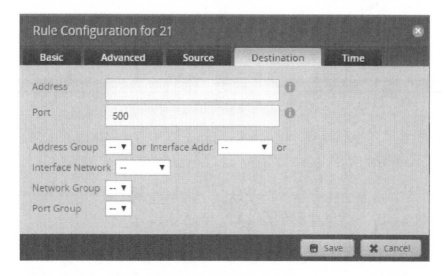

This is how the Basic screen should look.

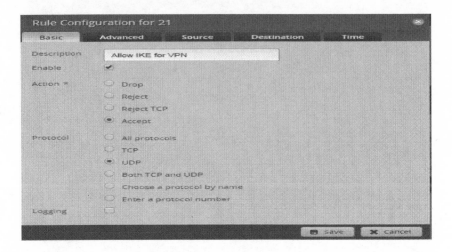

Make sure to click on the save button.

Let's add another rule. Same thing as before, click on new rule. Call this one "Allow L2TP for VPN."

Select Accept, and under the Protocol area again select UDP.

Click on the destination tab, and this time the destination port will be 1701.

Add yet another rule. Call this one "Allow Nat- Transversal."

Click the Accept button. Click the UDP selection again and on the Destination Tab enter the port 4500.

One more to go. Select new rule. Give it the description of "Allow ESP."

Click the Accept button. Now under the Protocol area, select Protocol by name, and once you find it, select ESP.

Click save.

Order	Description	Source	Destination	Protocol	Action	
	Ruleset Configuration for WAN_LOCAL					⊗
	Rules	Configuration	Interfaces	Stats		
1	Allow established/related			*	accept	Actions ▼
2	Drop invalid state			*	drop	Actions ▼
3	Allow IKE for VPN		port 500	udp	accept	Actions ▼
4	Allow L2TP for VPN		port 1701	udp	accept	Actions ▼
5	Allow Nat-Transversal		port 4500	udp	accept	Actions ▼
6	Allow ESP			esp	accept	Actions ▼

That's the final product. Let's review.

L2TP uses IPSEC to protect our data.

L2TP is more secure than PPTP.

You can set up a VPN without the use of a Radius Server.

You can do this!

It's a good idea once you have done all this, to go into the Config Tree, and look at your settings. Remember that you can use this utility to edit some of the parameters.

MTU SETTINGS

I don't really want to dig too deep here, but there is something you should know.

Not everything goes as planned.

What am I babbling about? Well one of the ways that routers trade data between each other is arriving at a correct size of the data packets that are whizzing back and forth. To do that they are doing what is called Path MTU discovery. To the beginner and frankly to most IT people in general, this whole process is mysterious. The sending and receiving routers agree on the best size of a packet by sending messages back and forth. They are attempting to agree on the optimal size of packet by starting off with the standard size of 1500 bytes. Then if the receiving device replies that the size is too large, then he replies with a message that instructs the sender to fragment the packet. You know, break it into smaller chunks so it fits through the pipe. This sounds like it should work perfectly. However it is not very reliable. The first problem is that the Protocol ICMP is used in sending the "Hey that's too big, send something smaller" messages. If that protocol is blocked by firewalls, or by devices on the internet, then you may see a huge slowdown of the data, to the point of failure. If it's a website the user is attempting to access, it may time out. Bad news.

You may need to change the MTU for a VPN to function correctly. Good luck doing that on an IPAD. You need to do this on the Router. A good work around to the problem is to set the TCP MSS Clamping on the router.

You can do this in the Wizard section. You would set the Segment size to a lower number than 1500. Start with 1492. You could go much lower and it would still work. But at some point you would be sending too many small packets. You can also do this in the CLI. If you followed the example above, you just need to add the line.

```
# Set vpn l2tp remote-access mtu 1492
```

This is actually a pretty common issue. Different vendors will suggest different MTU values to set. Some will suggest 1460 like our buddies at Mikrotik and Cisco, and some will suggest even smaller values to support proprietary devices.

It's a very easy thing to set up in the wizard or in the CLI. It just may not always be needed.

Well, that's a wrap. See you all in Volume2.

Appendix

GLOSSARY

ACCESS METHOD: Generally, the way in which network devices access the network medium. CSMA C/D, Polling.

ACK: Acknowledgment. Notification sent from one network device to another to acknowledge that some event has occurred. Sometimes abbreviated ACK.

ADAPTER: Network Interface Card. NIB. Ethernet Adapter.

ADDRESS MASK: Bit combination used to describe which portion of an address refers to the network or subnet and which part refers to the host. Sometimes referred to simply as mask. Either written as 255.255.255.0 or the CIDR equivalent of /24.

ADDRESS RESOLUTION: Generally, a method for resolving differences between computer addressing schemes. Address resolution usually specifies a method for mapping network layer (Layer 3) addresses to data link layer (Layer 2) addresses.

ADJACENCY: Relationship formed between selected neighboring routers and end nodes for the purpose of exchanging routing information. Adjacency is based upon the use of a common media segment. And is also formed when Routers share the same Area ID#, Authentication, Dead and Hello Timer values.

ADMINISTRATIVE DISTANCE: A rating of the trustworthiness of a routing information source. In routers, administrative distance is expressed as a numerical value between 0 and 255. The higher the value, the lower the trustworthiness rating.

AGENT: 1) Generally, software that processes queries and returns replies on behalf of an application. 2) In NMSs, process that resides in all managed devices and reports the values of specified variables to management stations. 3) Maxwell Smart.

ALGORITHM: 1) Well-defined rule or process for arriving at a solution to a problem. In networking, algorithms are commonly used to determine the best route for traffic from a particular source to a particular destination. 2) Former Vice-President attempting to maintain a rhythm.

AREA: Logical set of network segments (usually OSPF- based) and their attached devices. Areas are usually connected to other areas via routers, making up a single autonomous system.

ARP: Address Resolution Protocol. Internet protocol used to map an IP address to a MAC address. This is Broadcast traffic. Pretty chatty too.

ASBR: Autonomous System Boundary Router. An ASBR is located between an OSPF autonomous system and a non-OSPF network. ASBRs run both OSPF and another routing protocol, such as RIP.

AUTONOMOUS SYSTEM: Collection of networks under a common administration sharing a common routing strategy. Autonomous systems are subdivided by areas. An autonomous system is assigned a unique 16-bit number by the IANA.

ASBR: Autonomous system boundary router. ABR located between an OSPF autonomous system and a non-OSPF network. ASBRs run both OSPF and another routing protocol, such as RIP. ASBRs must reside in a nonstub OSPF area.

BACKBONE: 1) The part of a network that acts as the primary path for traffic that is most often sourced from, and destined for, other networks. 2) Main pathway for High speed data links. 3) Area of Anatomy that some politicians lack.

BANDWIDTH: The difference between the highest and lowest frequencies available for network signals. The term is also used to describe the rated throughput capacity of a given network medium or protocol.

BIT: Binary digit used in the binary numbering system. Can be 0 or 1.

BLACK HOLE: Routing term for an area of the internetwork where packets go in, but do not come out, due to Network problems or poor system configuration within a portion of the network. This can also be configured as a security measure to send packets to a perceived destination that in fact does not exist. Also Tarpit.

BRIDGE: Device that connects and passes packets between two network segments that use the same communications protocol. Bridges operate at the data link layer (layer 2) of the OSI reference model. In general, a bridge will filter, forward, or flood an incoming frame based on the MAC address of that frame. Also the linking of interfaces such as wireless and wired to form one entity.

BRIDGE GROUP: Feature that assigns network interfaces to a particular spanning-tree group. Also mating multiple interfaces together as a switch/bridge.

BROADCAST ADDRESS: A Special address reserved for sending a message to all stations. Generally, a broadcast address is a MAC destination address of all ones. Compare with multicast address and unicast address.

BROADCAST DOMAIN: The set of all devices that will receive broadcast frames originating from any device within the set. Broadcast domains are typically bounded by routers because routers do not forward broadcast frames. Routers will not forward a Broadcast.

BROADCAST STORM: Undesirable network event in which many broadcasts are sent simultaneously across all network segments. A broadcast storm uses substantial network bandwidth and can slow your network to the point of failure. It's all bad.

BUFFER: Storage area used for handling data in transit. Buffers are used in internetworking to compensate for differences in processing speed between network devices. Bursts of data can be stored in buffers until they can be handled by slower processing devices. Sometimes referred to as a packet buffer.

BYTE: Term used to refer to a series of consecutive binary digits that are operated upon as a unit (for example, an 8-bit byte) Half of a Byte is a nibble. No I'm not kidding. Look it up!

CIRCUIT: Communications path between two or more points.

CLI: Command-line interface.

COLLISION: In Ethernet, the result of two nodes transmitting simultaneously. The frames from each device impact and are damaged when they meet on the physical media. In Ethernet networks collisions are handled by CSMA/CD. For wireless networks the protocol CSMA/CA is used.

COLLISION DOMAIN: In Ethernet, the network area within which frames that have collided are propagated. Repeaters and hubs propagate collisions; LAN switches, bridges and routers do not. Donate your hubs to one of the "STAN" countries.

COMMAND-LINE INTERFACE: Aka the CLI.

CONCENTRATOR: Multi-port repeater, or a HUB.

CONTENTION: Access method in which network devices compete for permission to access the physical medium. Contrast with circuit switching and token passing.

CONVERGENCE: The speed and ability of a group of internetworking devices running a specific routing protocol to agree on the topology of an internetwork after a change in that topology. Fast is good!

COST: Arbitrary or random value, which is typically based on hop count, media bandwidth, or other measures, that is assigned by a network administrator and used to compare various paths through an internetwork environment. Cost values are used by routing protocols to determine the most favorable path to a particular destination: the lower the cost, the better the path. Sometimes called path cost.

CPE: Customer premises equipment. Terminating equipment, such as terminals, telephones, and modems, supplied by the telephone company, installed at customer sites, and connected to the telephone company network.

CPU: Central processing unit. The part of a computer that controls all the other parts, sometimes called the Brain. It fetches instructions from memory and decodes them.

CSMA/CD: Carrier sense multiple access with collision detect. Media-access mechanism wherein devices ready to transmit data first check the channel for a carrier. If no carrier is sensed for a specific period of time, a device can transmit. If two devices transmit at once, a collision occurs and is detected by all colliding devices. This collision subsequently delays retransmissions from those devices for some random length of time. CSMA/CD access is used by Ethernet wired devices.

DARPA: Defense Advanced Research Projects Agency. The U.S. government agency that funded research for and experimentation with the Internet.

DATAGRAM: Information sent as a network layer unit over a transmission medium without prior establishment of a virtual circuit. IP datagrams are the primary information units in the Internet. The terms frame, message, packet, and segment are also used to describe Information at various layers of the OSI reference model.

DATA LINK LAYER: Layer 2 of the OSI reference model. This layer provides reliable transit of data across a physical link. The data link layer is concerned with physical addressing, network topology, line discipline, error notification, ordered delivery of frames, and flow control. The IEEE has divided this layer into two sub layers: the MAC sub layer and the LLC sub layer.

DEDICATED LAN: A Network segment allocated to one single device. Used in LAN switched network topologies.

DEFAULT ROUTE: Routing table entry that is used to direct frames for which a next hop is not explicitly listed in the routing table.

GLOSSARY

DELAY: The time between the initiation of a transaction by a sender and the first response received by the sender. Also, the time required to move a packet from source to destination over a given path.

DESIGNATED ROUTER: OSPF router that generates LSAs for a OSPF network and has other special responsibilities in running OSPF. Each multi access OSPF network that has at least two attached routers has a designated router that is elected by the OSPF Hello protocol. The designated router enables a reduction in the number of adjacencies required on a multi access network, which in turn reduces the amount of routing protocol traffic and the size of the topological database.

DIJKSTRA'S ALGORITHM: Shortest path first algorithm. Routing algorithm that iterates on length of path to determine a shortest-path spanning tree. Commonly used in link-state routing algorithm. OSPF=Link State.

DISTANCE VECTOR: Routing algorithm Class of routing algorithms that iterate on the number of hops in a route to find a shortest-path spanning tree. Distance vector routing algorithms call for each router to send its entire routing table in each update, but only to its neighbors. Distance vector is used for the Routing Protocol RIP. This Protocol has largely been replaced by OSPF. (Routing Information Protocol) Rest in Peace.

DNS: Domain Naming System. System used in the Internet for translating names of network nodes into addresses. So when you type in the name, you will arrive at an address.

DOT ADDRESS: Refers to the common notation for IP addresses in the form where each number written, in decimal, 1 byte of the 4-byte IP address. Also called dotted notation or four part dotted notation. EX. 192.168.1.1.

DYNAMIC ROUTING: Routing that adjusts automatically to network topology or traffic changes. Absolute wizardry.

ETHERNET: Baseband LAN specification invented by Xerox Corporation and developed jointly by Xerox, Intel, and Digital Equipment Corporation. Ethernet networks use CSMA/CD and runs over a variety of media types at 10 Mbps.

EVENT: Network message indicating operational irregularities in physical elements of a network or a response to the occurrence of a given task, typically the completion of a request for information. See also alarm and trap.

FAST ETHERNET: Any of a number of 100-Mbps Ethernet specifications. Fast Ethernet offers a speed increase ten times that of the 10BASET Ethernet specification, while still doing basic functions as frame formatting, MAC mechanisms, and MTU. Such similarities allow the use of existing 10BASE-T applications and network management tools on Fast Ethernet networks. Based on an extension to the IEEE 802.3 specification.

FORWARDING: Process of sending a frame toward its ultimate destination by way of an internetworking device. That device could be a switch or a router.

FRAGMENT: Piece of a larger packet that has been broken down to smaller unit

FRAME: Logical grouping of information sent as a data link layer unit over a transmission medium. Often refers to the header and trailer, used for synchronization and error control. The terms datagram, message, packet, and segment are also used to describe the Frame (DATA) at various layers of the OSI reference model.

FULL DUPLEX: Capability for simultaneous data transmission between a sending station and a receiving station. Basically sending and receiving at the same time.

GATEWAY: In the IP community, an older term referring to a routing device. Today, the term router is used to describe nodes that perform this function. The term gateway is a bit generic. It signals a transition, and that transition can be from one protocol to another, or one cable type to another.

HALF DUPLEX: Capability for data transmission in only one direction at a time between a sending station and a receiving station. Like a walkie-talkie.

HARDWARE ADDRESS: A 48 bit address, that is burned in, or programmed to be permanent on your network adapter. Written in Hexadecimal format.

HELLO: Multicast packet that is used by routers for neighbor discovery and recovery. Hello packets also indicate that a client is still operating and network- ready.

HERTZ: Measure of frequency, abbreviated Hz. Synonymous with cycles per second.

HEXADECIMAL: Base 16. A number representation using the digits 0 through 9, with their usual meaning, plus the letters A through F to represent hexadecimal digits with values of 10 to 15. The rightmost digit counts ones, the next counts multiples of 16, then $16^2=256$, etc.

HOP COUNT: Routing metric used to measure the distance between a source and a destination. RIP uses hop count as its sole metric. Each link to a neighboring Router is one hop. By using only Hop count the router could not tell if the link was a fast or slow one. In contrast OSPF uses the Metric of Bandwidth/Delay, meaning it will look at the speed of the Link. If there is the same speed on more than one route, OSPF will go to the second metric of delay, and using ICMP it will gauge the latency of each connection, and will choose the fastest one available.

HOST: Computer system on a network. Similar to the term node except that host usually implies a computer system, whereas node generally applies to any networked system, including access printers, servers and routers.

HOST ADDRESS: Part of an IP address that designates which node on the subnet is being addressed.

HUB: Multi port repeater. It finds the destination of each addressed frame by broadcasting to each port. Replaced by switches.

IANA: Internet Assigned Numbers Authority. IANA delegates authority for IP address-space allocation. IANA also maintains a database of assigned protocol identifiers used in the TCP/IP stack, including autonomous system numbers.

IEEE: Institute of Electrical and Electronics Engineers. Professional organization whose activities include the development of communications and networking standards. IEEE LAN standards are the predominant LAN standards today. To work there you must own a pocket protector.

INTERFACE: 1) Connection between two systems or devices. 2) In routing terminology, a network connection. 3) The boundary between adjacent layers of the OSI model.

INTERNET: Term used to refer to the largest global internetwork, connecting tens of thousands of networks worldwide. The Internet evolved in part from ARPANET. At one time, called the DARPA Internet.

IP: Internet Protocol. The big Kahuna of Protocols. It is a Network layer protocol in the TCP/IP stack offering a connectionless internetwork service. IP provides features for addressing, type-of-service specification, fragmentation and reassembly, and security.

IP ADDRESS: 1) 32-bit address assigned to hosts using TCP/IP. An IP address belongs to one of five classes (A, B, C, D, or E) and is written as 4 octets separated with periods (dotted decimal format). Each address consists of a network number, an optional subnetwork number, and a host number. The network and subnetwork numbers together are used for routing, while the host number is used to address an individual host within the network or subnetwork. A subnet mask is used to extract network and subnetwork information from the IP address.

JABBER: An error condition in which a network device continually transmits random, meaningless data onto the network. This means that your network card or adapter is failing, or has failed.

LAN: Local-area network. Generally a High-speed, low- error data network. LANs connect workstations, printers, servers, and other devices in a single building or other geographically limited area. LAN standards specify cabling and signaling at the physical and data link layers of the OSI model.

LAN SWITCH: High-speed switch that forwards packets between data-link segments.

LASER: Light amplification by stimulated emission of radiation. Never point it at your eyeball!

LATENCY: 1) Delay between the times a device requests access to a network and the time it is granted access to transmit. 2) Delay between the time when a device receives a frame and the time that frame is forwarded out the destination port.

LED: Light emitting diode. Semiconductor device that emits light produced by converting electrical energy. Status lights on hardware devices are typically LEDs. This one you can look at!

LINK STATE ROUTING ALGORITHM: Routing algorithm in which each router broadcasts or multicasts information regarding the cost of reaching each of its neighbors to all nodes in the internetwork.

LOAD BALANCING: In routing, the ability of a router to distribute traffic over all its network ports that are the same distance from the destination address. Load balancing increases the utilization of network segments, thus increasing effective network bandwidth.

MAC ADDRESS: Also known as a hardware address, a MAC-layer address, or a physical address. Compare with network address.

MODEM: Modulator-Demodulator. Device that converts digital and analog signals. At the source, a modem converts digital signals to a form suitable for transmission over analog communication facilities. At the destination, the analog signals are returned to their digital form. Modems allow data to be transmitted over voice-grade telephone lines. I believe Hell still uses Dialup.

MTU: Maximum Transmission Unit. Maximum packet size, in bytes, that a particular interface can handle.

MULTICAST ADDRESS: Single address that refers to multiple network devices. Synonymous with group address.

NAK: Negative Acknowledgment. Response sent from a receiving device to a sending device to let them know that the information received contained errors.

NAME SERVER: Server connected to a network that resolves network names into network addresses.

NET: Short for network. Nothing but.

NETWORK: Collection of computers, printers, routers, switches, and other devices that are able to communicate with each other over some transmission medium.

NETWORK ADDRESS: Network layer address referring to a logical, rather than a physical, network device. Your devices IP address.

NETWORK INTERFACE: Boundary between at least two dissimilar networks.

NETWORK LAYER: Layer 3 of the OSI reference model. This layer provides connectivity and path selection between two end systems. The network layer is the layer at which routing occurs.

NETWORK MANAGEMENT: Generic term used to describe systems or actions that help maintain, or troubleshoot a network.

NETWORK NUMBER: Part of an IP address that specifies the network to which the host belongs.

NETWORKING: Connecting of any collection of computers, printers, routers, switches, and other devices for the purpose of communication over a transmission medium.

NIC: Network Interface Card. Board that provides network communication capabilities. Also called a NIB

NMS: Network Management System. System responsible for managing parts of a network. An NMS is generally a program running on a server. NMSs communicate with agents to help keep track of network statistics and resources.

NODE: Node is sometimes used generically to refer to any entity that can access a network, and is frequently used interchangeably with device.

OSI REFERENCE MODEL: Open System Interconnection reference model. Network architectural model developed by ISO. International Standards Org.

OSPF: Open Shortest Path First. Link-state, hierarchical IGP routing algorithm that is a successor to RIP in the Internet community. OSPF features include least-cost routing, multipath routing, and load balancing.

PACKET: Logical grouping of information that includes a header containing control information and (usually) user data. Packets are most often used to refer to network layer units of data. Routers move Packets, Switches move frames.

PHYSICAL LAYER: Layer 1 of the OSI reference model.

PING: Short for Packet Internet Groper, a utility to determine whether a specific IP address is accessible. It works by sending a packet to the specified address and waiting for a reply. PING is used primarily to troubleshoot Internet connections. Runs as a utility under the protocol ICMP.

POLICY ROUTING: Routing scheme that forwards packets to specific interfaces based on user-configured policies. Such policies might specify that traffic sent from a particular network should be forwarded out one interface, while all other traffic should be forwarded out another interface. Heavily involves the firewall.

POLLING: Access method in which a primary network device inquires, in an orderly fashion, whether other devices have data to transmit.

PORT: 1) Interface on an internetworking device (such as a router). 2) In IP terminology, an upper-layer process that is receiving information from lower layers. 3) To rewrite software or code so that it will run on a different hardware platform or in a different software environment than that for which it was originally designed. 4). A female plug on a patch panel or a switch which accepts the same size plug as an RJ45 jack. 5) Grandma Wine.

PRESENTATION LAYER: Layer 6 of the OSI reference model.

PROTOCOL: Formal description of a set of rules and conventions that govern how devices on a network exchange information.

PROXY ARP: Proxy Address Resolution Protocol. Variation of the ARP protocol in which an intermediate device (for example, a router) sends an ARP response on behalf of an end node to the requesting host. Proxy ARP can reduce bandwidth use on slow speed WAN links.

QOS: Quality of Service. Measure of performance for a transmission system that reflects its transmission quality and service availability.

QUEUE: A set of rules or routines to apply policies to traffic types, protocols, or ports.

RADIUS: Remote Authentication Dial-In User Service is a networking protocol that provides centralized Authentication, Authorization, and Accounting management.

RIP: Routing Information Protocol. At one point it was the most common interior gateway protocol in the Internet. RIP uses hop count as a routing metric. Also known as a Distance Vector Protocol. What's your vector Victor?

ROUTE: Path through an internetwork.

ROUTED PROTOCOL: Protocol that can be routed by a router. A router must be able to interpret the logical internetwork as specified by that routed protocol. Examples of routed protocols include AppleTalk, and IP.

ROUTER: Network layer device that uses one or more metrics to determine the optimal path along which network traffic should be forwarded. Routers forward packets from one network to another based on network layer information. Sometimes called a gateway.

GLOSSARY

ROUTING: Process of finding a path to a destination host.

ROUTING METRIC: Method by which a routing algorithm determines that one route is better than another. This information is stored in routing tables. Metrics include bandwidth, communication cost, delay, hop count, load, MTU, path cost, and reliability. Sometimes referred to simply as a metric.

ROUTING PROTOCOL: Protocol that accomplishes routing through the implementation of a specific routing algorithm. Examples of routing protocols include IGRP, OSPF, and RIP.

ROUTING TABLE: Table stored in a router that keeps track of routes to particular network destinations and, in some cases, metrics associated with those routes.

SEGMENT: Section of a network that is bounded by bridges, routers, or switches.

SESSION LAYER: Layer 5 of the OSI reference model. This layer establishes, manages, and terminates sessions between applications and manages data exchange between presentation layer entities.

SHOW IP ROUTE: Command that displays the contents of an IP routing table.

SOURCE ADDRESS: Address of a network device that is sending data.

STATIC ROUTE: Route that is explicitly configured and entered into the routing table. Static routes generally take precedence over routes chosen by dynamic routing protocols.

SUBNET MASK: 32-bit address mask used in IP to indicate the bits of an IP address that are being used for the subnet address. Sometimes referred to simply as mask.

SWITCH: Network device that filters, forwards, and floods frames based on the destination address of each frame. The switch operates at the data link layer of the OSI model.

TCP/IP: Transmission Control Protocol/Internet Protocol. Common name for the suite of protocols developed by the U.S. DoD in the 1970s to support the construction of worldwide internetworks. TCP and IP are the two best-known protocols in the suite.

THROUGHPUT: Rate of information arriving at, and possibly passing through, a particular point in a network system.

TOPOLOGY: Physical arrangement of network nodes and media within an enterprise networking structure.

TRAFFIC SHAPING: Use of queues to limit or restrict data types, or larger flows of traffic. Can be used to restrict speeds based on ports or applications.

TRANSPORT LAYER: Layer 4 of the OSI reference model. This layer is responsible for reliable network communication between end nodes.

UNICAST: Message sent to a single network destination.

VLAN: Virtual LAN. Group of devices on a LAN that are configured (using management software) so that they can communicate as if they were attached to the same wire, when in fact they are located on a number of different LAN segments. Because VLANs are based on logical instead of physical connections, they are extremely flexible.

WAN: Wide-area network. Data communications network that serves users across a geographical or logical boundary.

Made in the USA
Lexington, KY
31 January 2019